FABULOUS FASHIONS

COLORING BOOK

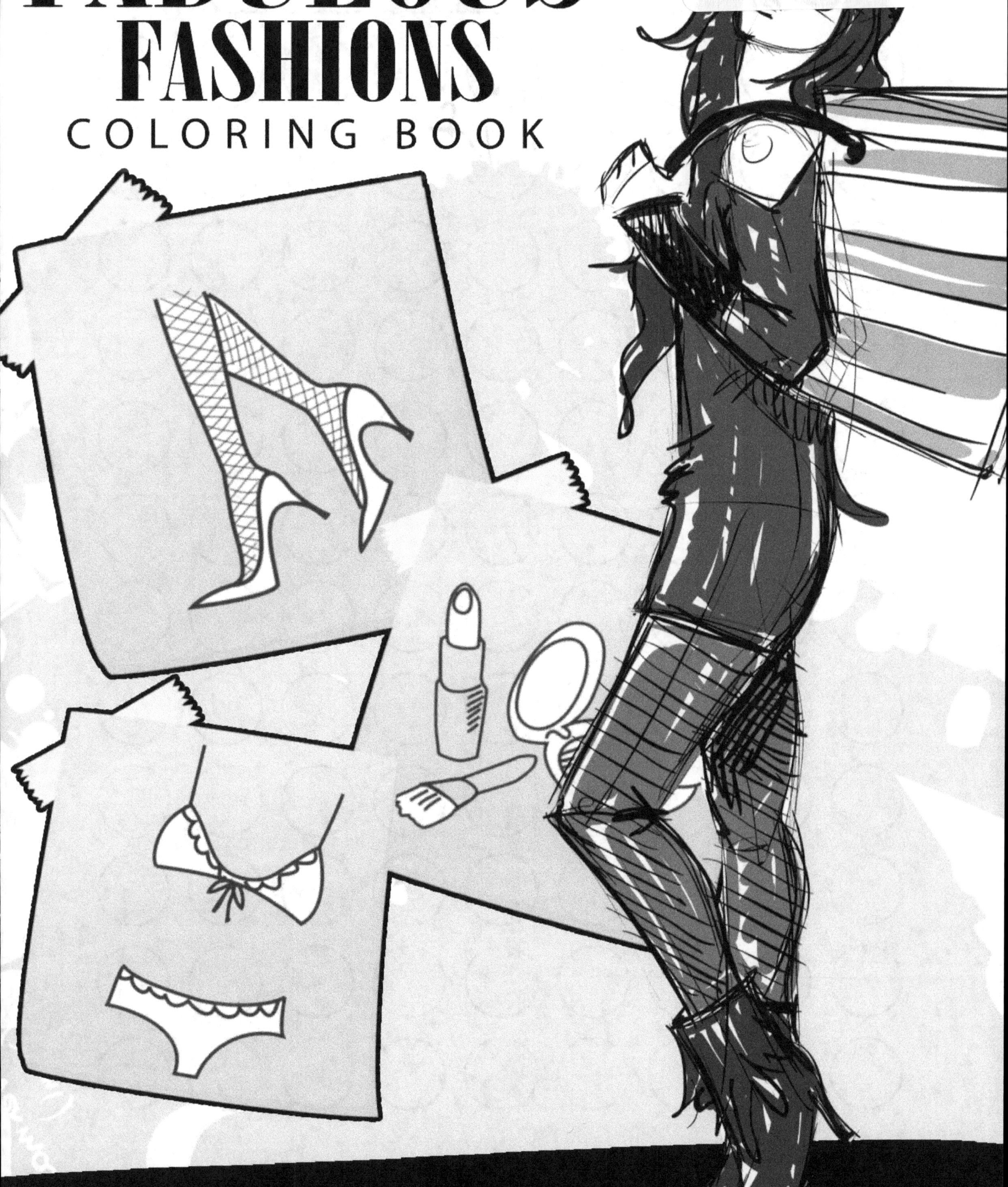

COLOR TEST PAGE

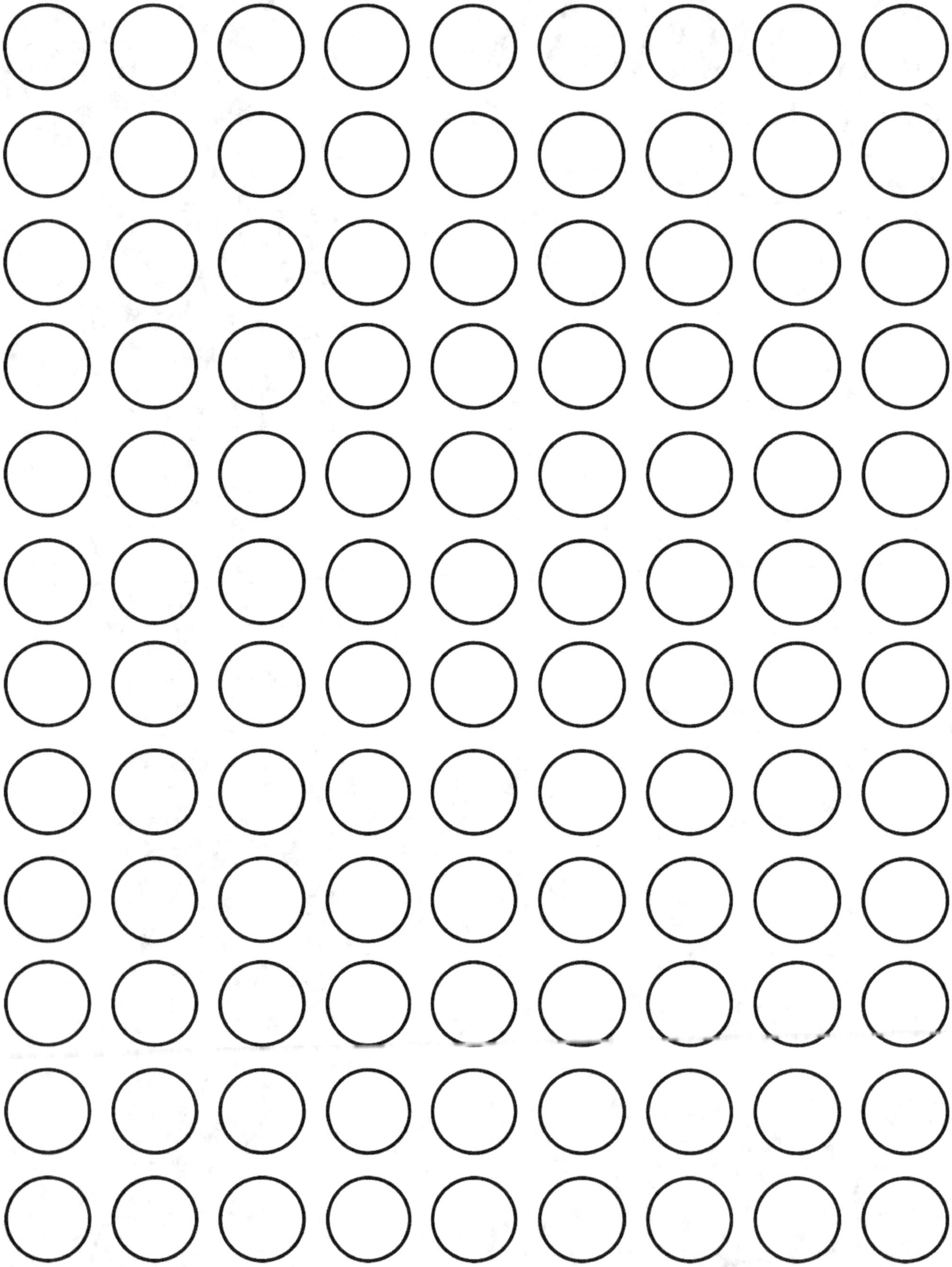

COLOR TEST PAGE

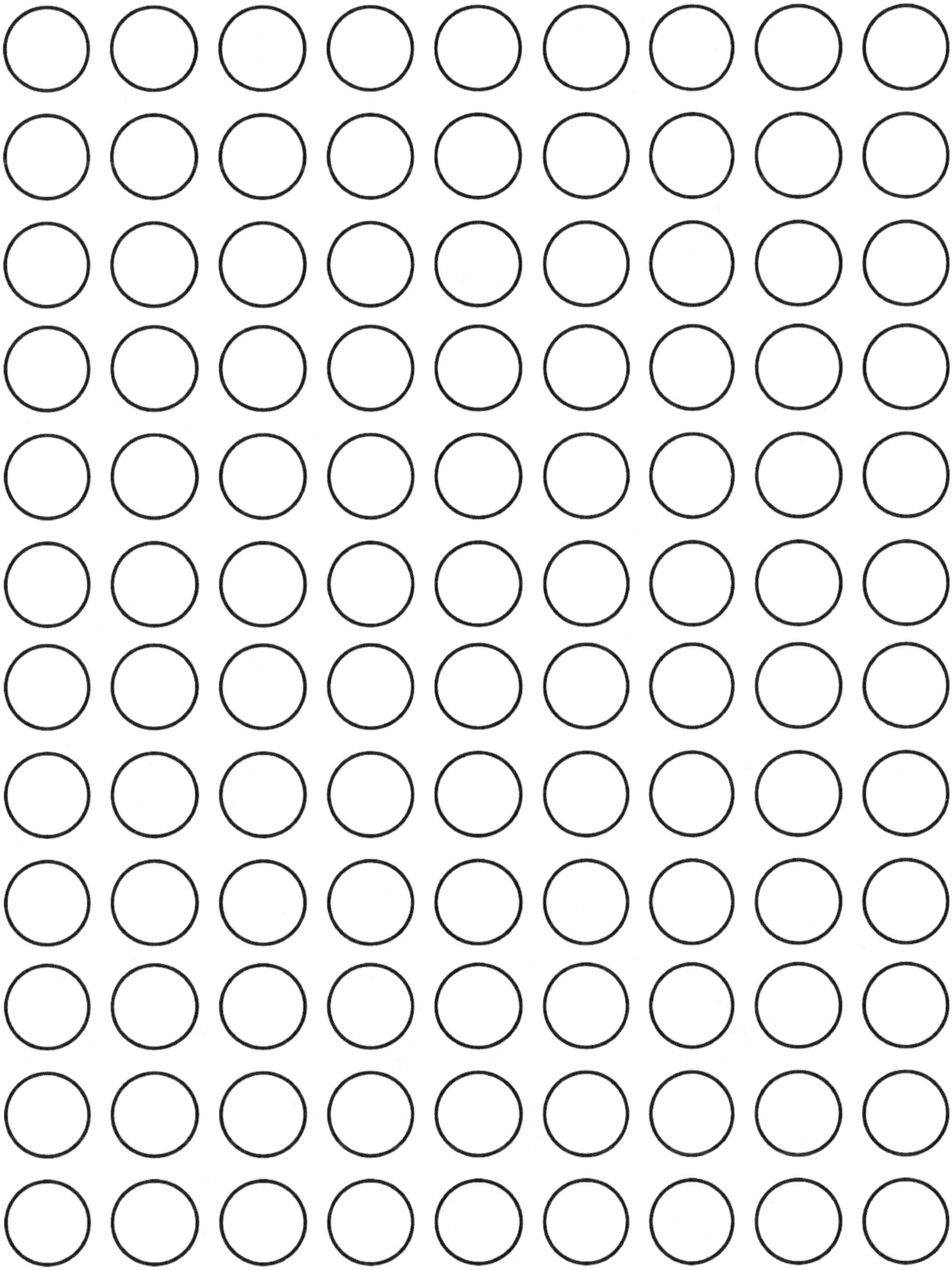

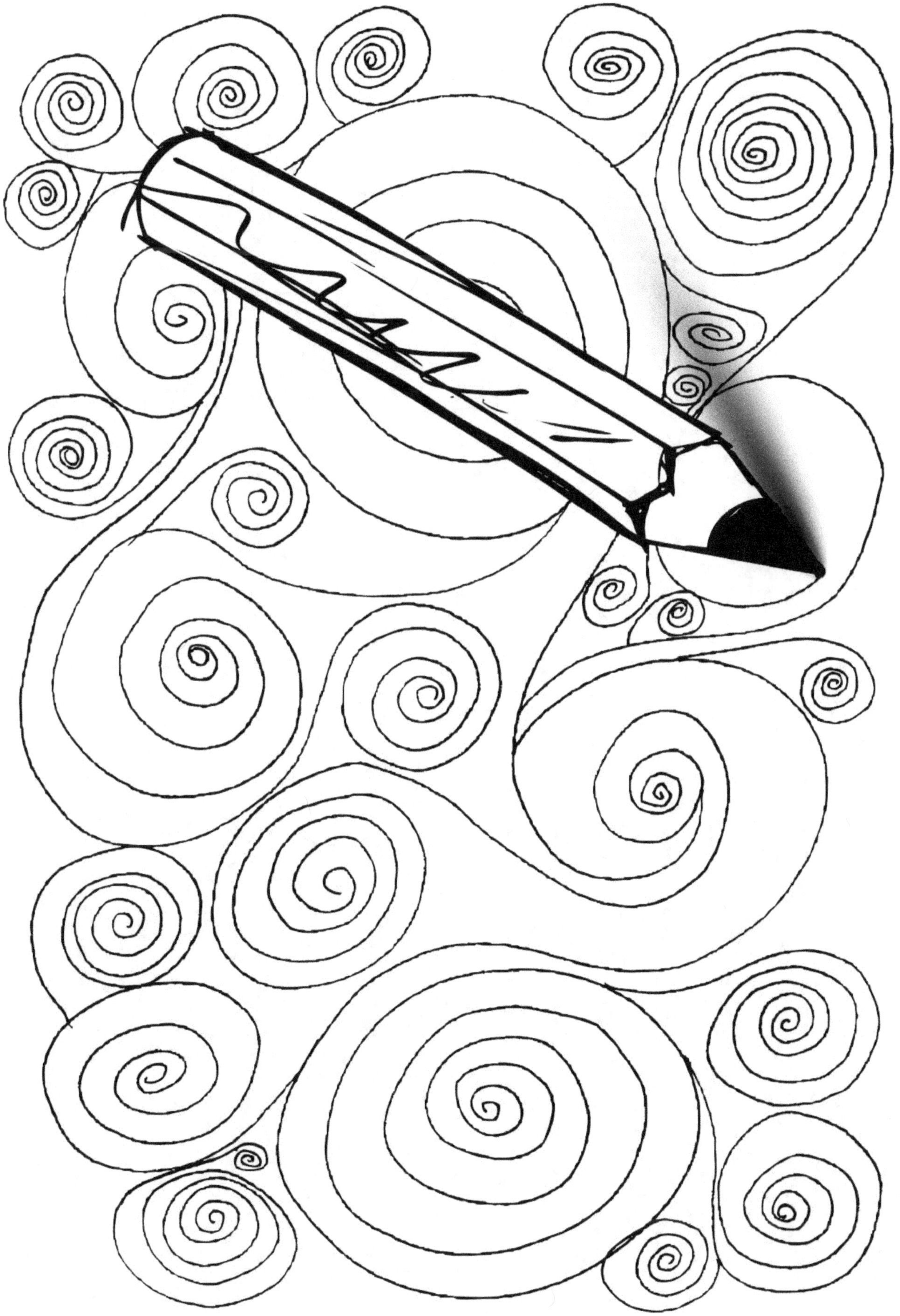

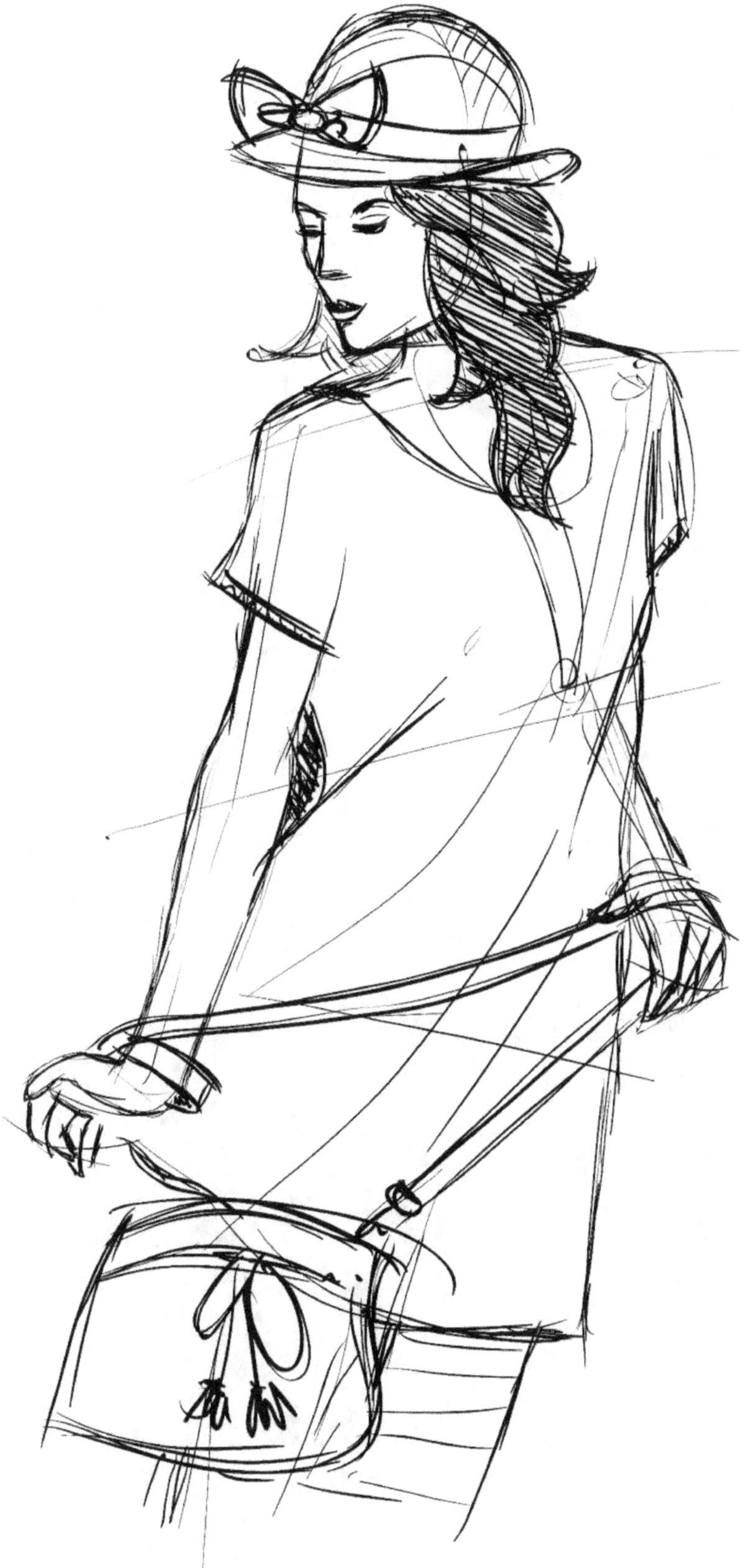

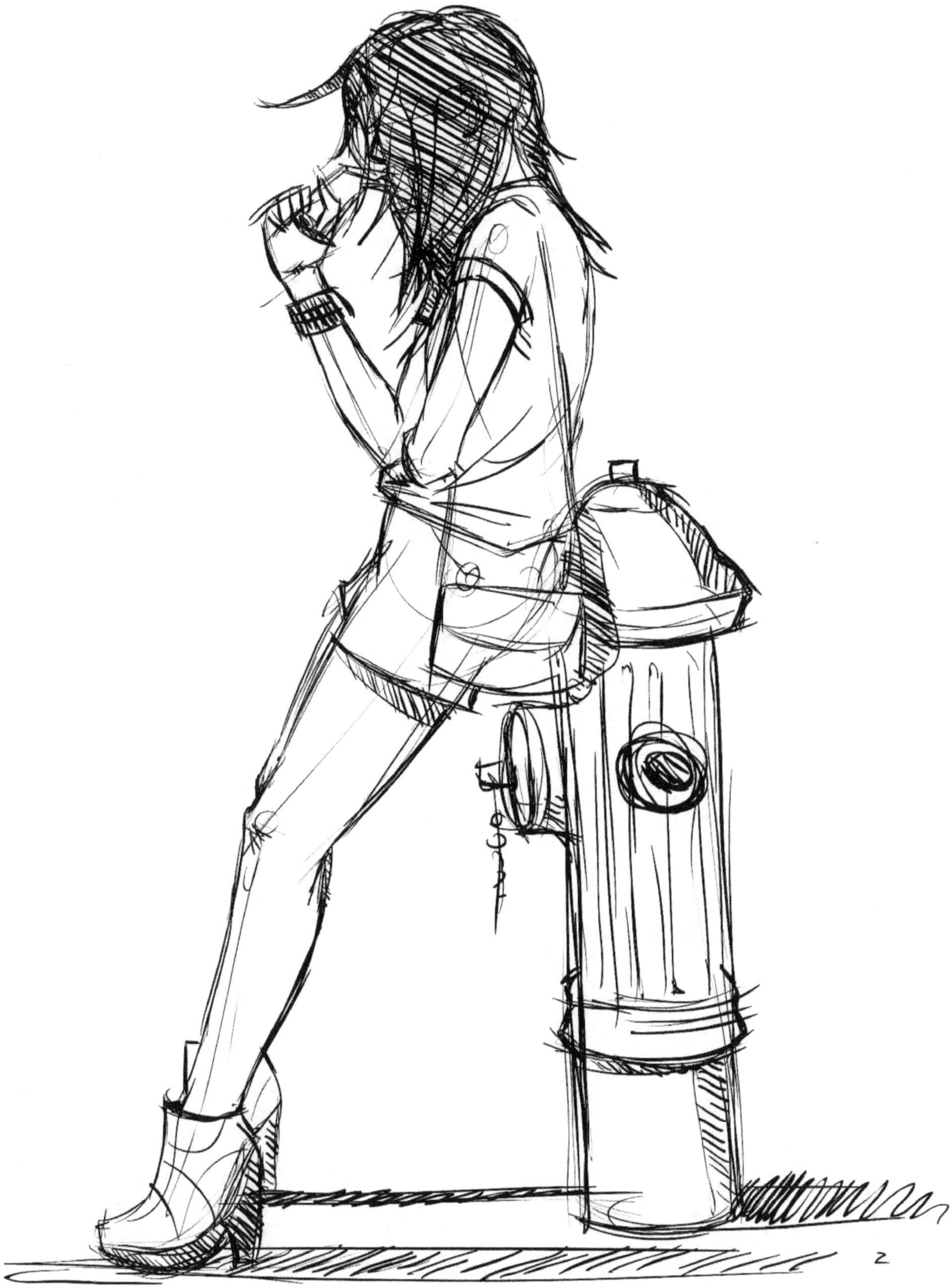

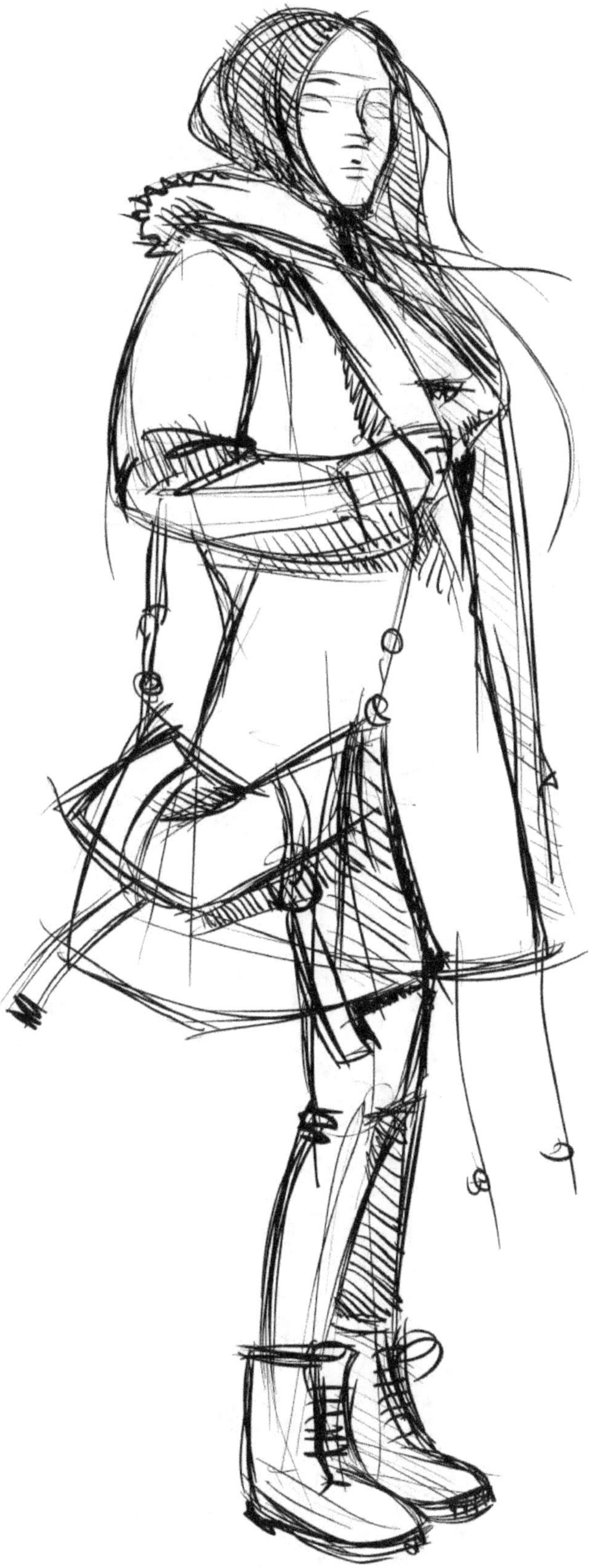

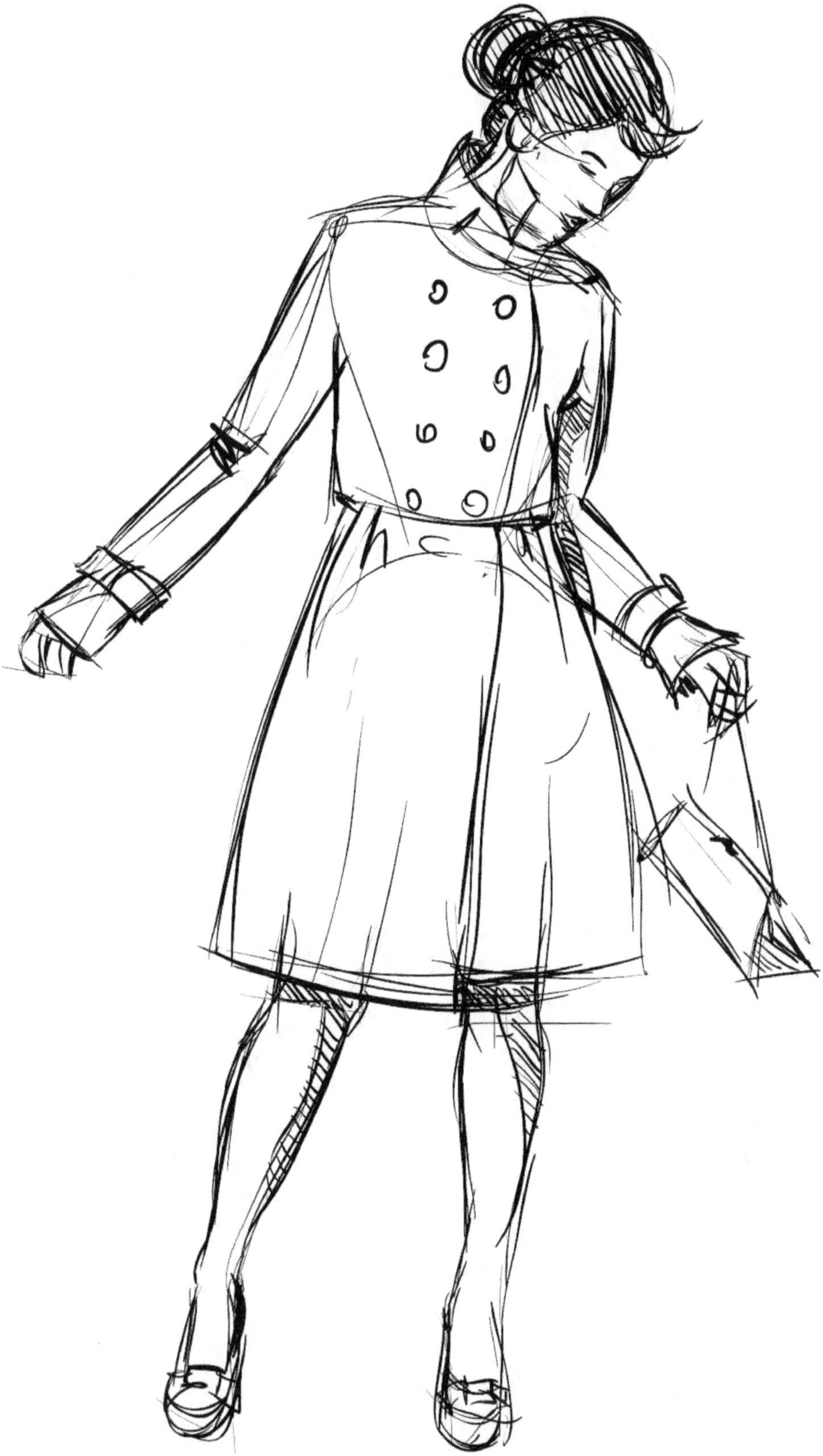

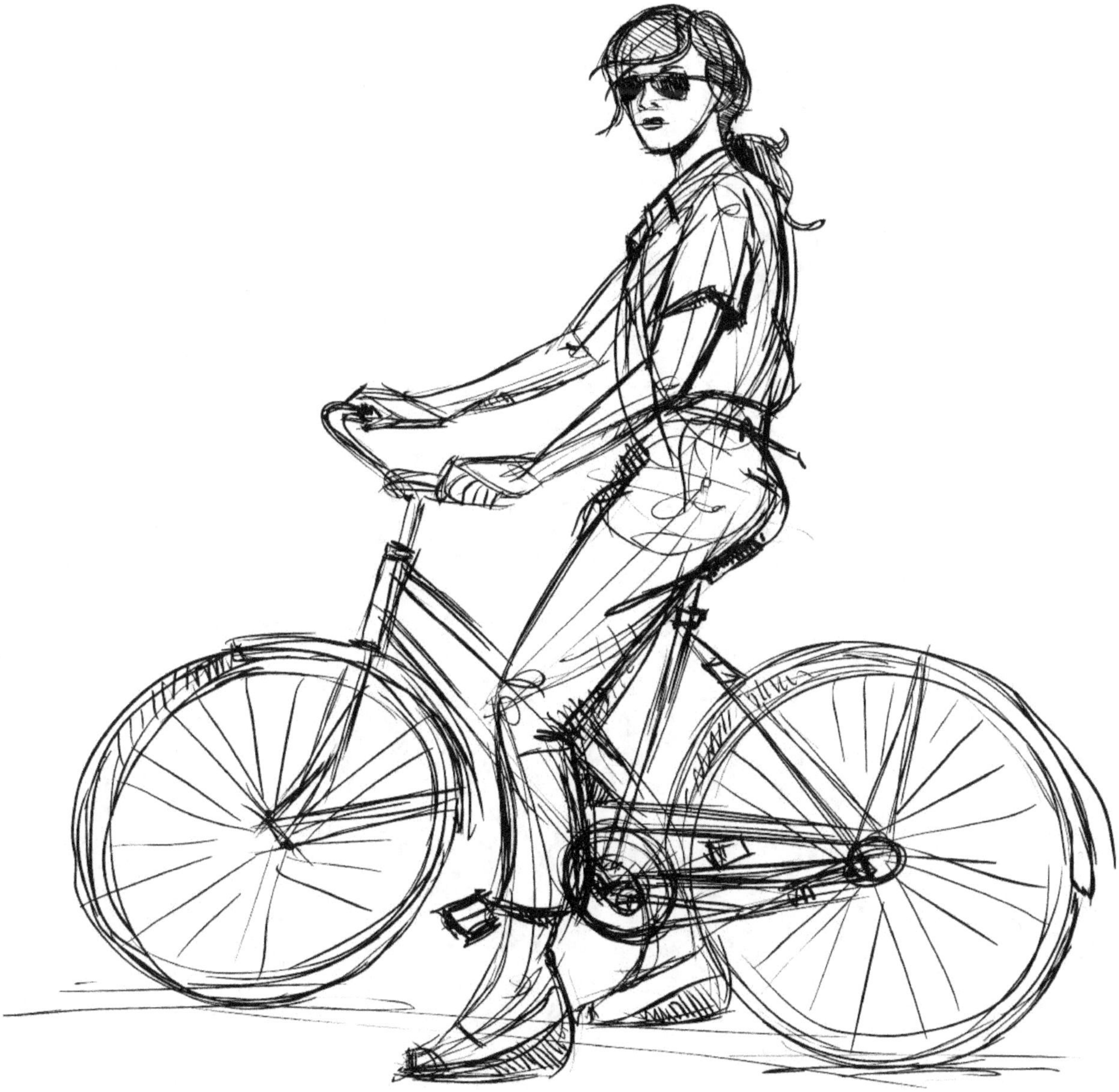

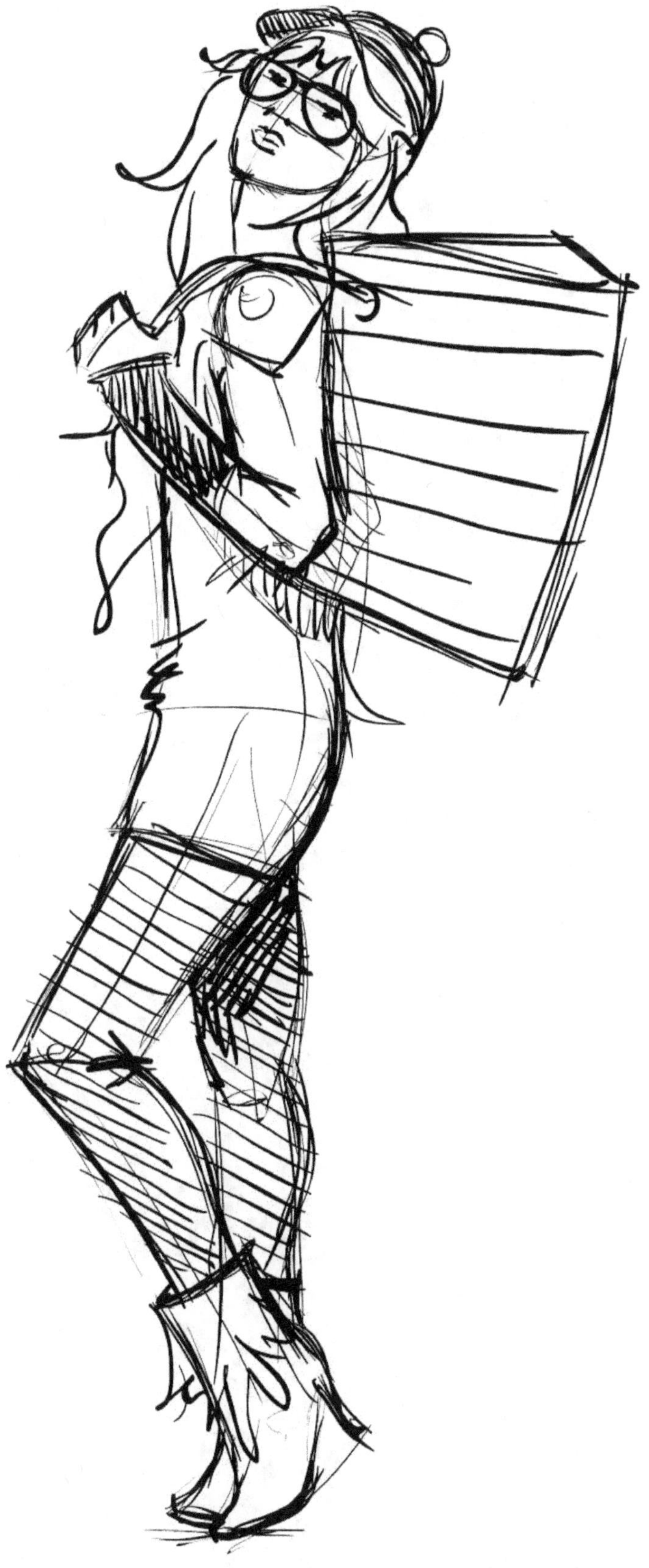

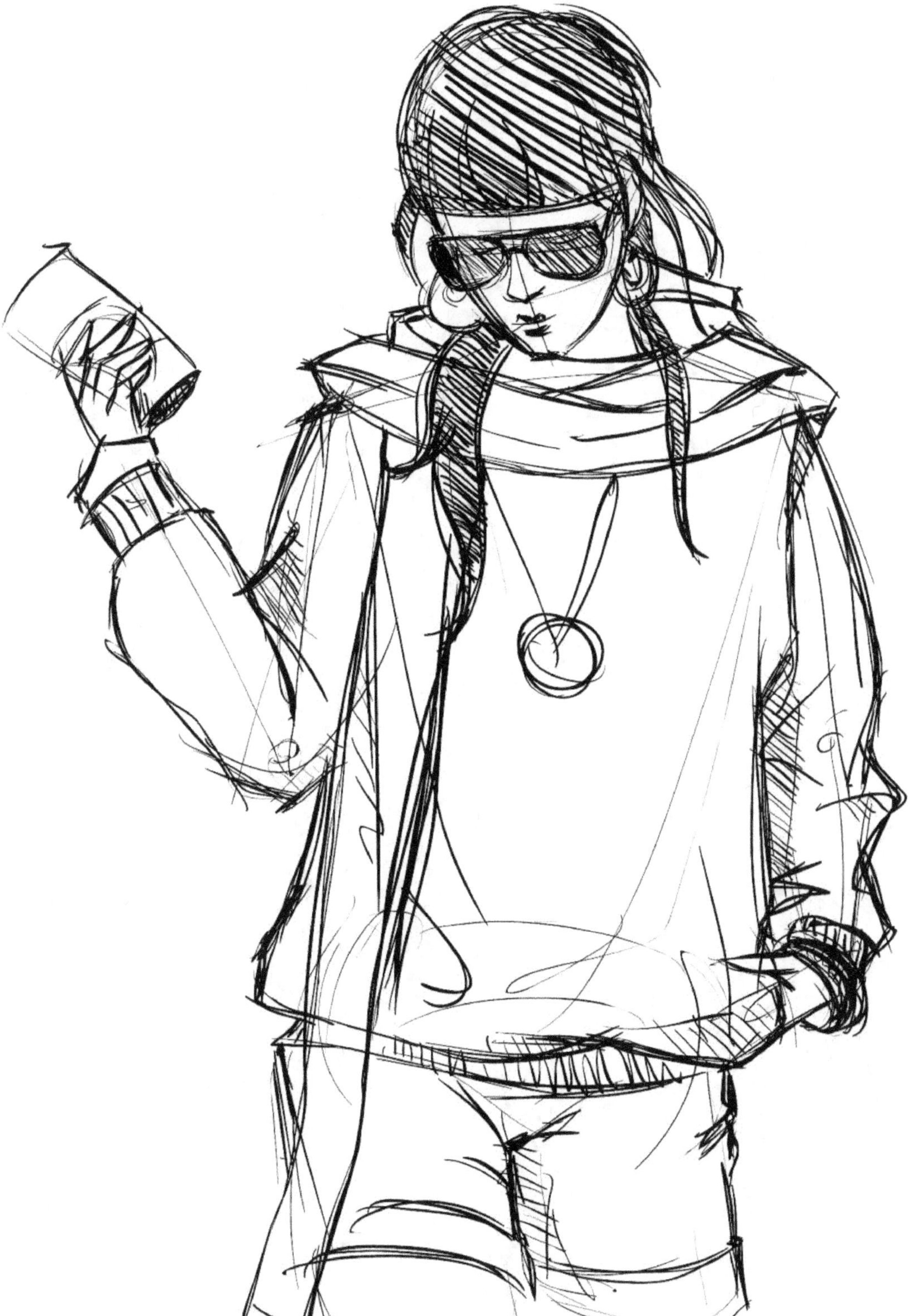

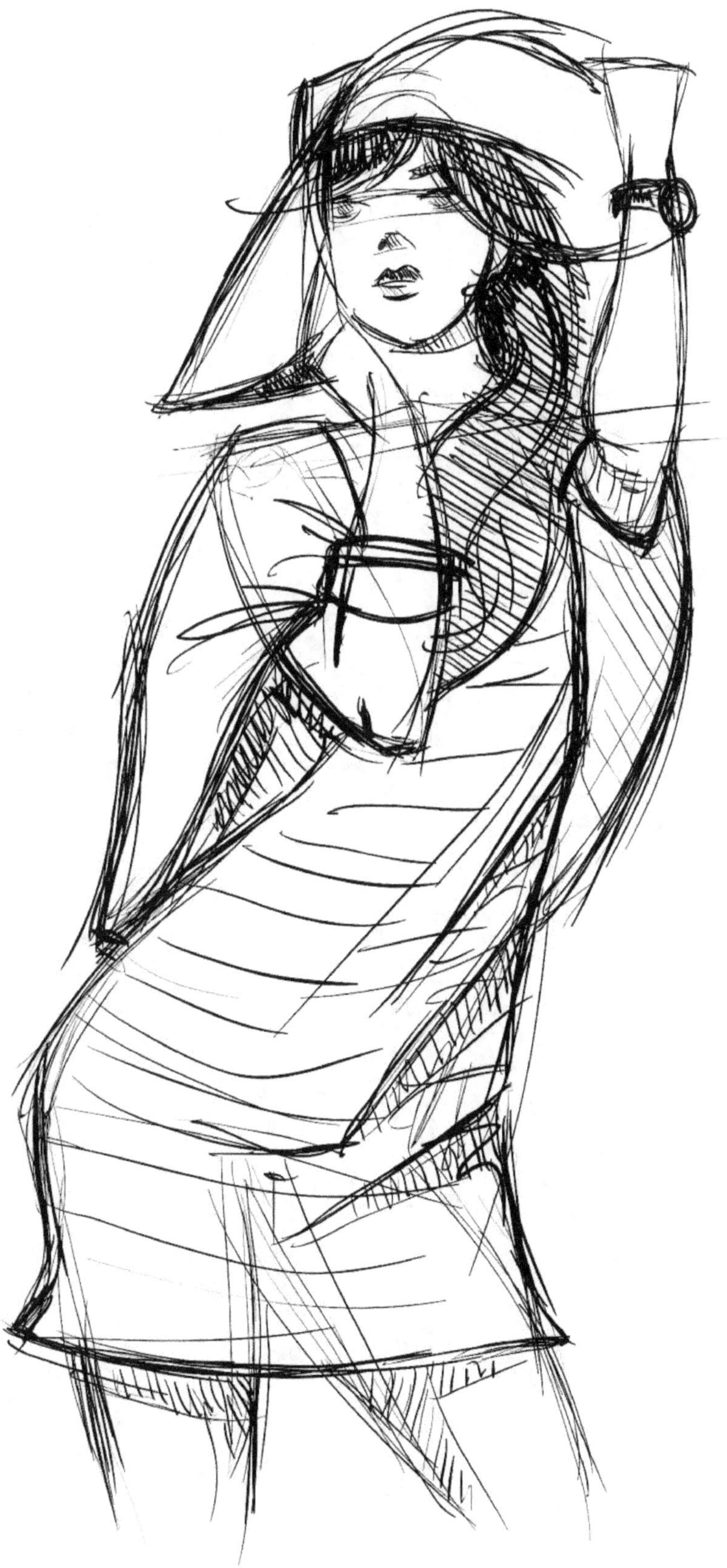

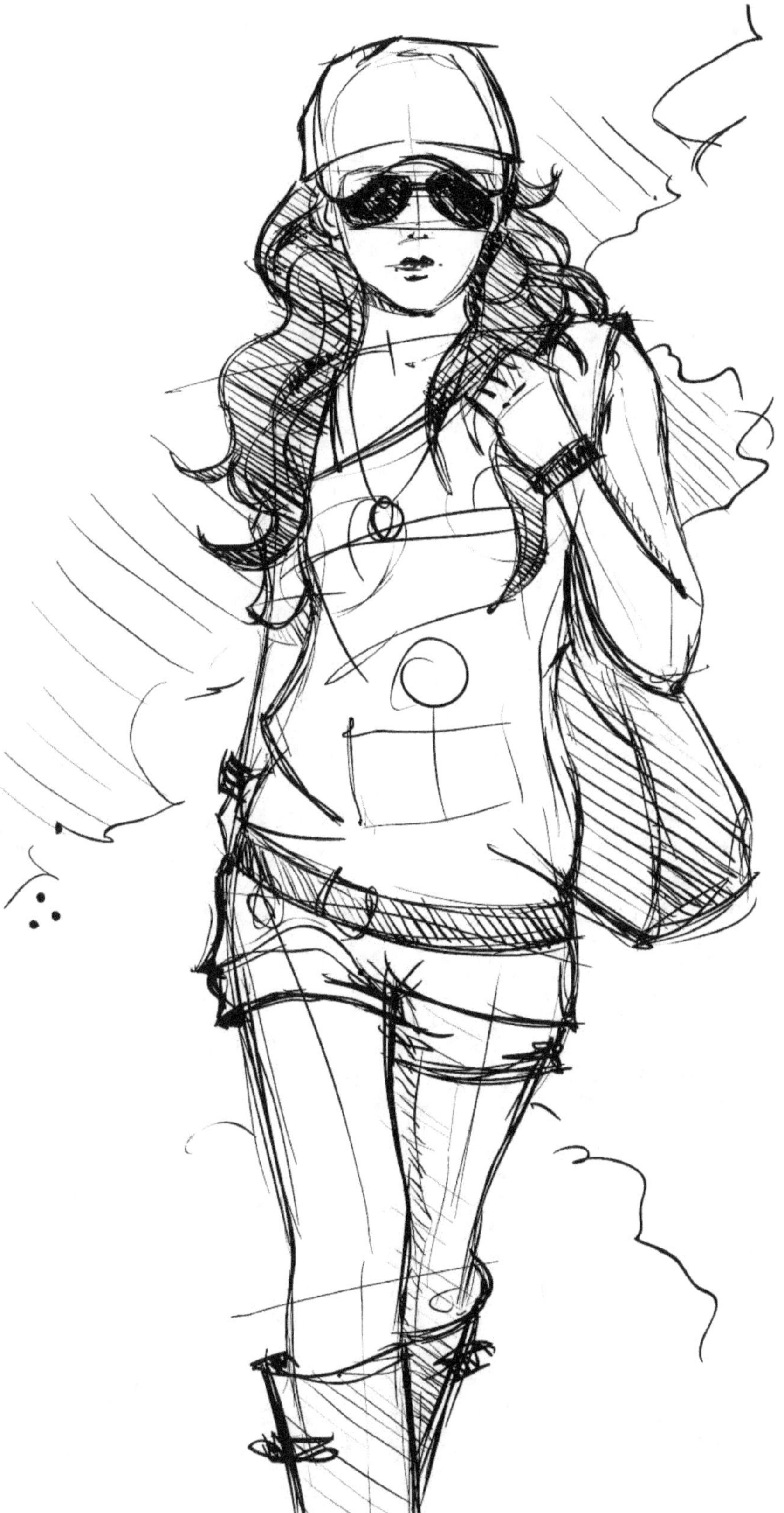

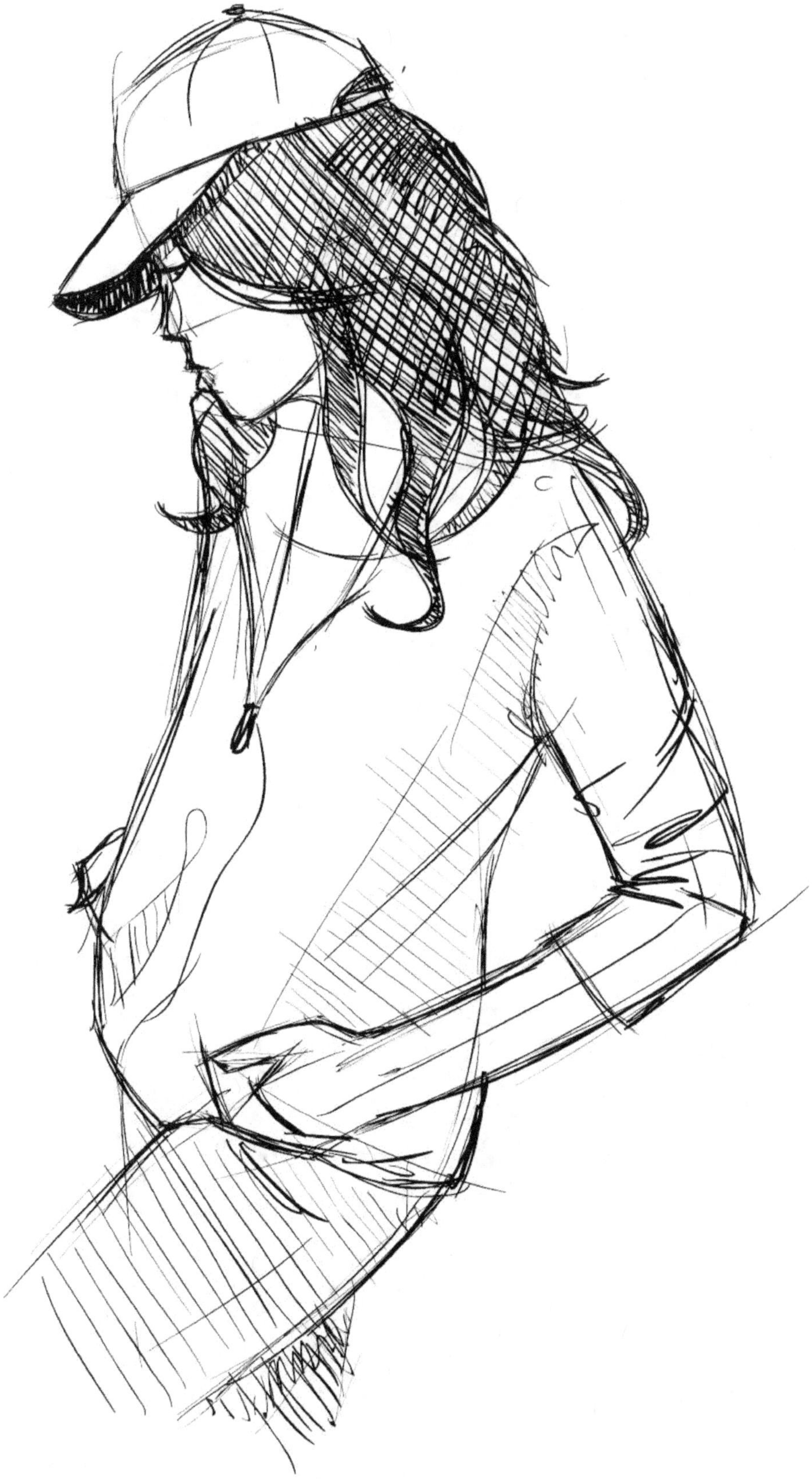

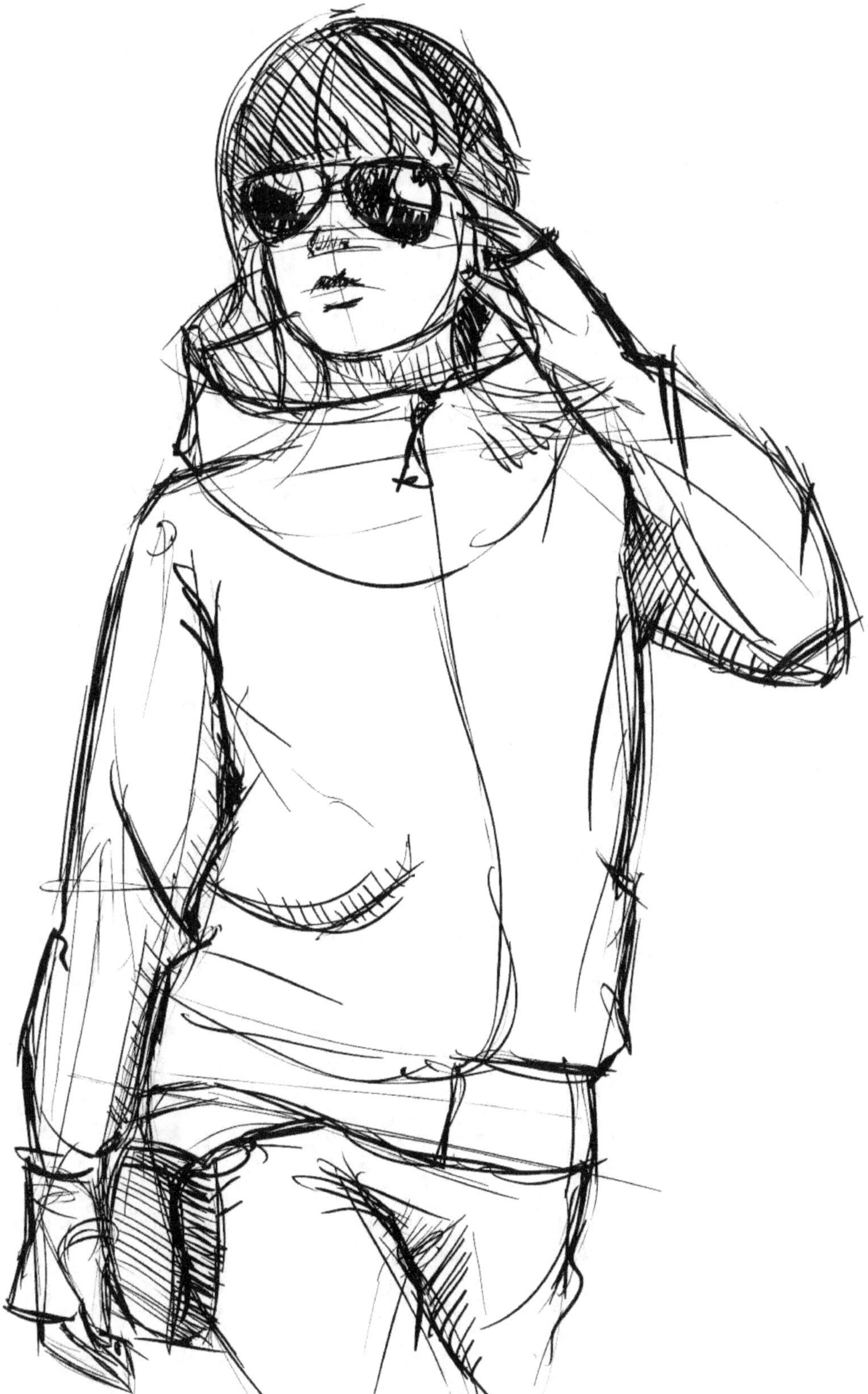

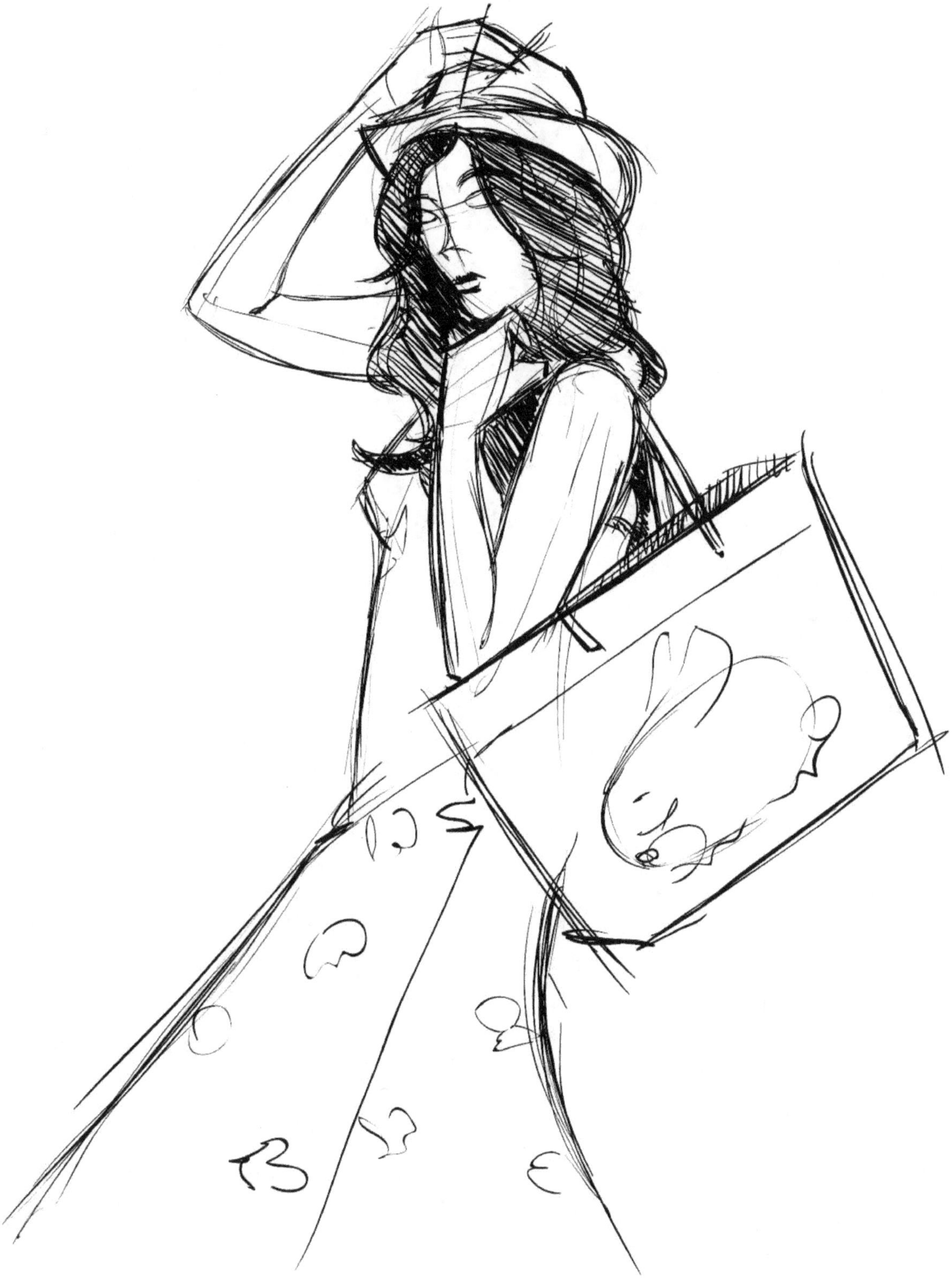

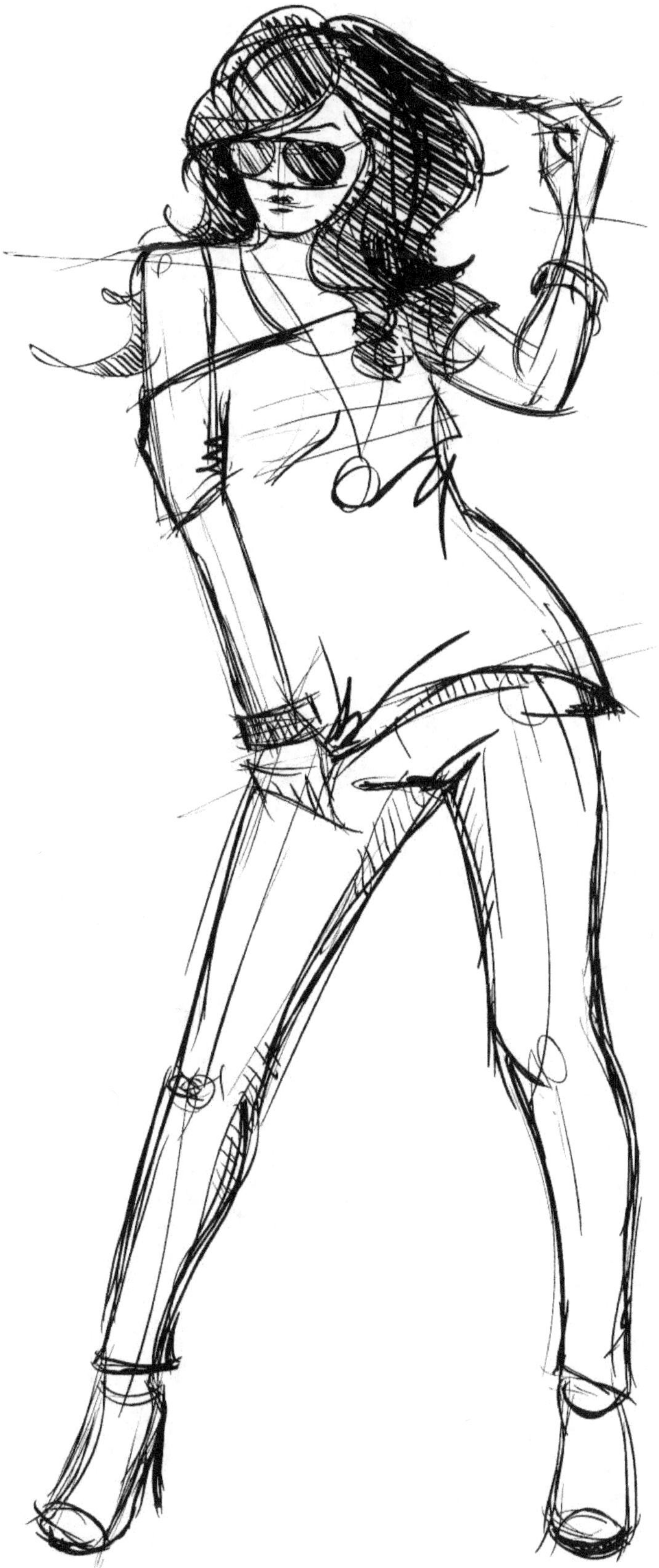

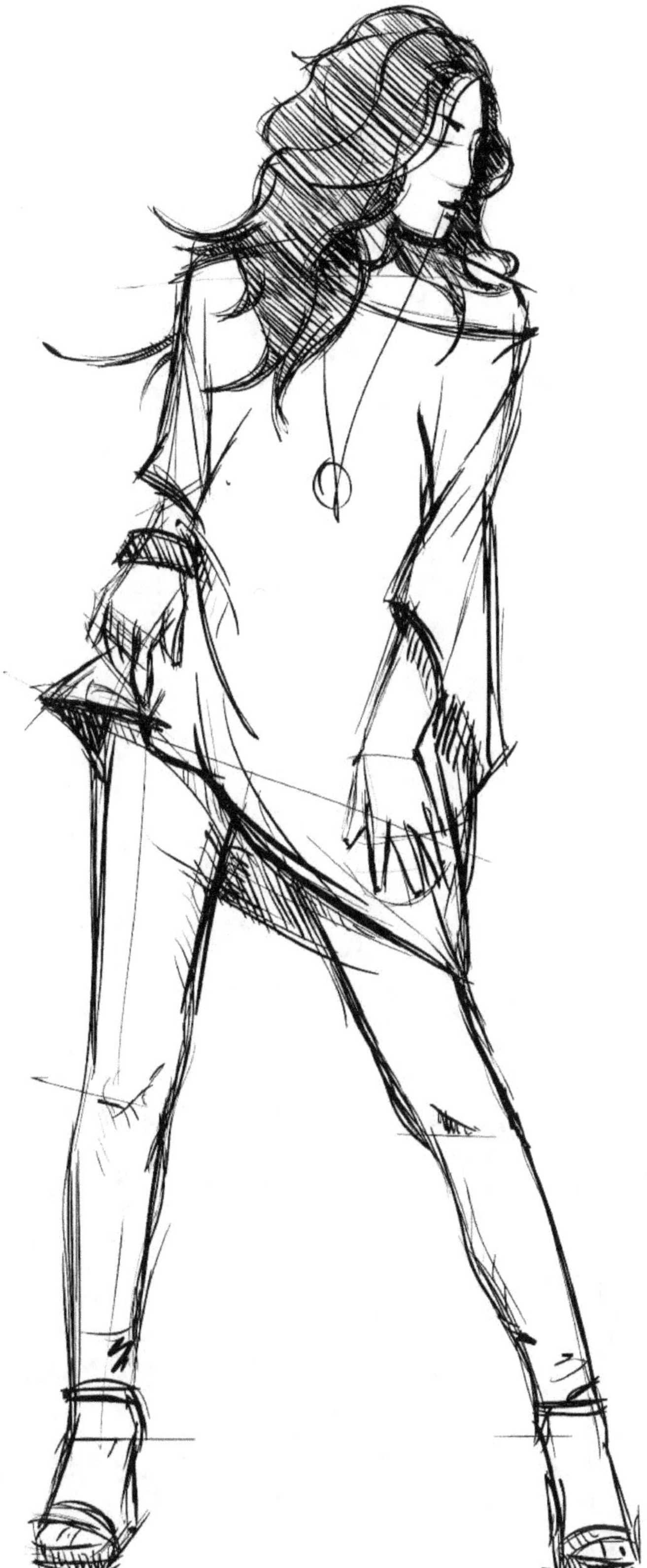

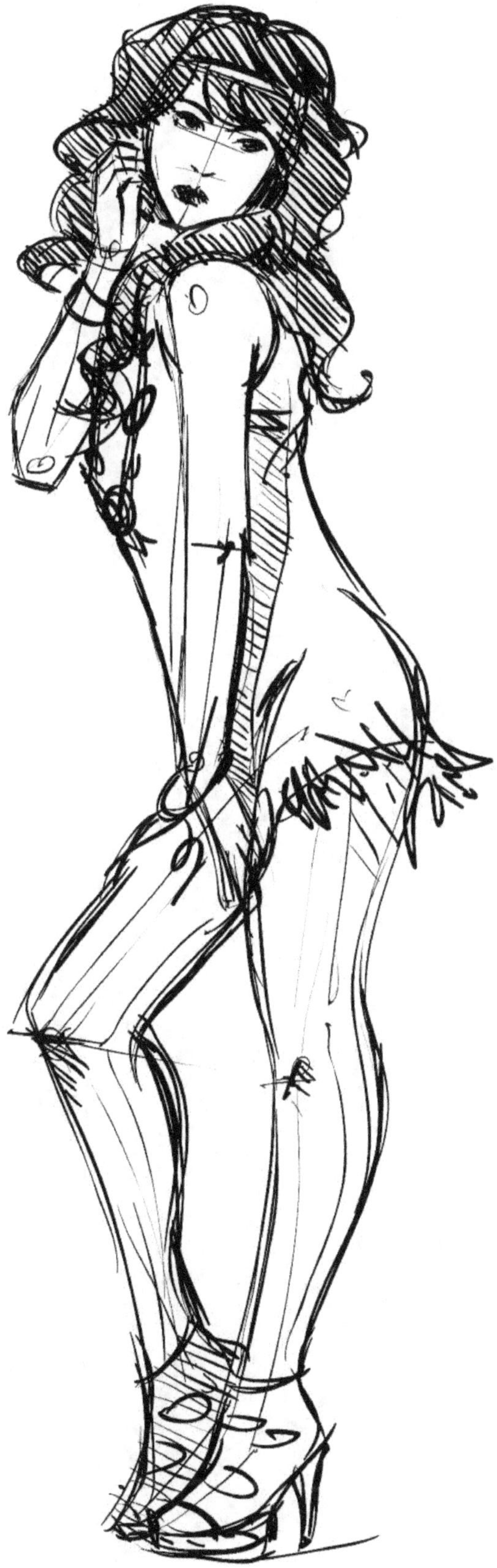

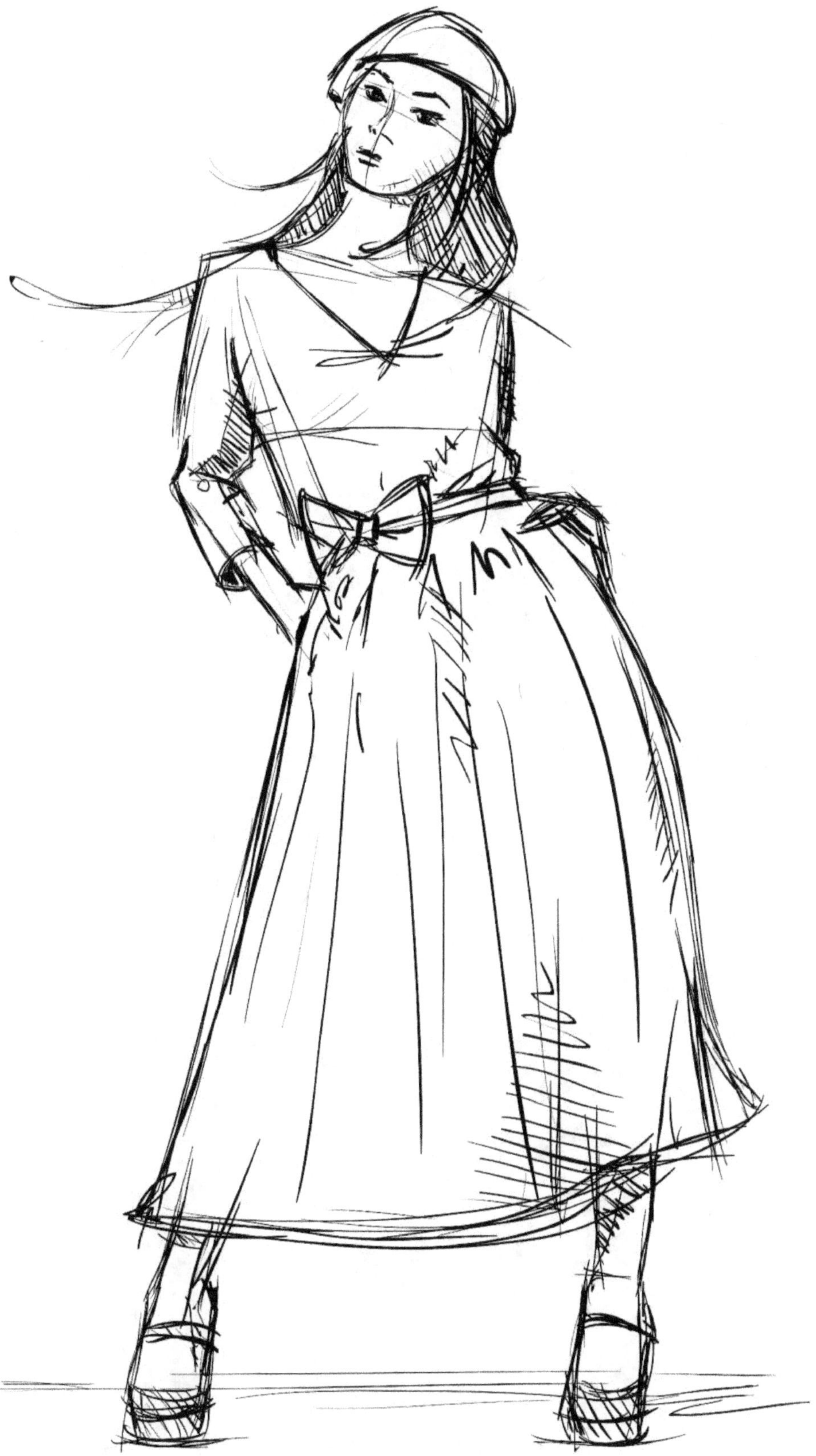

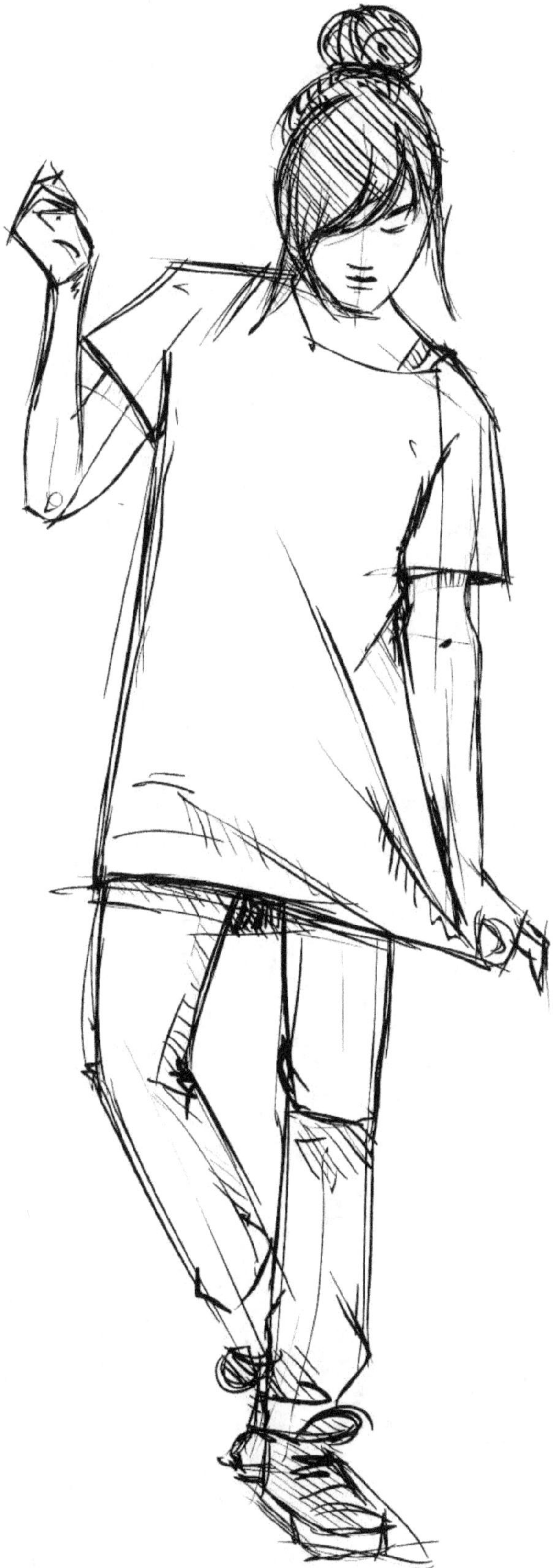

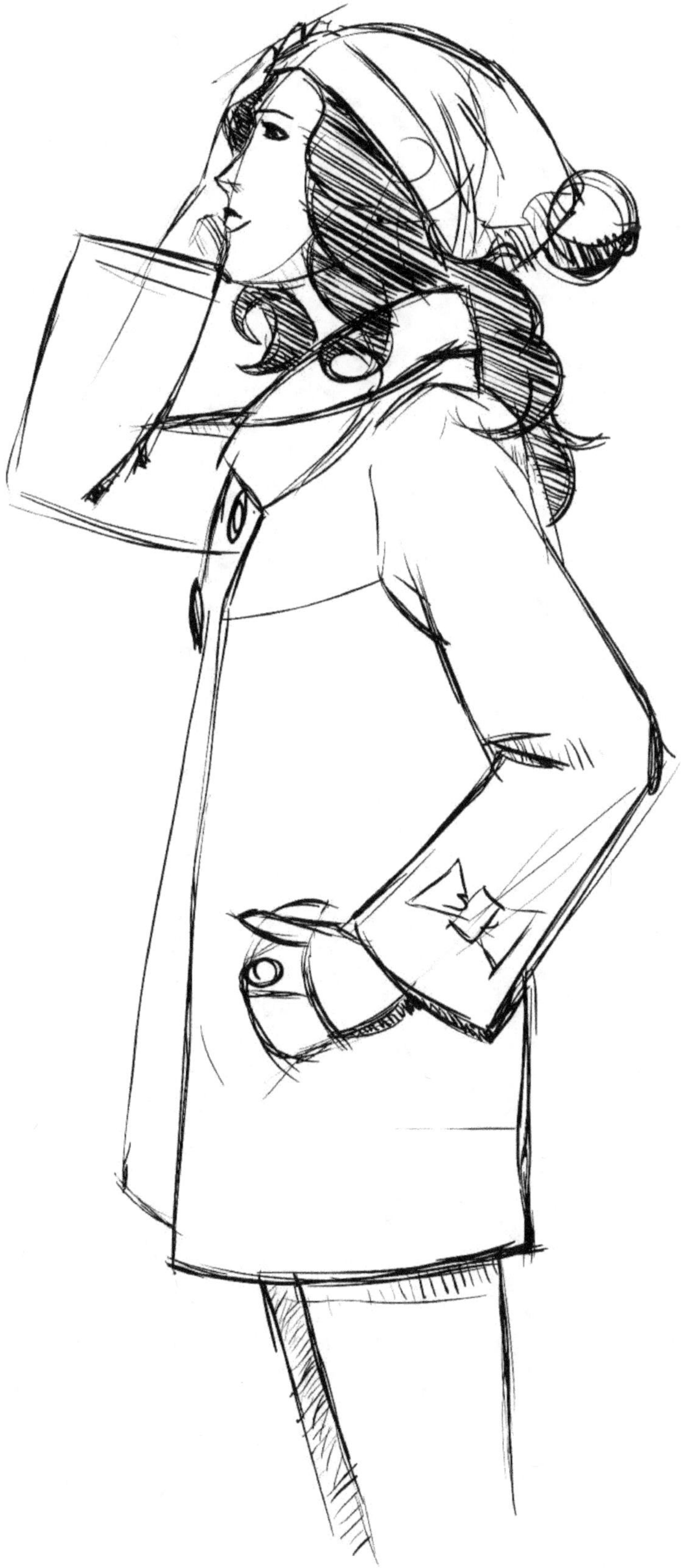

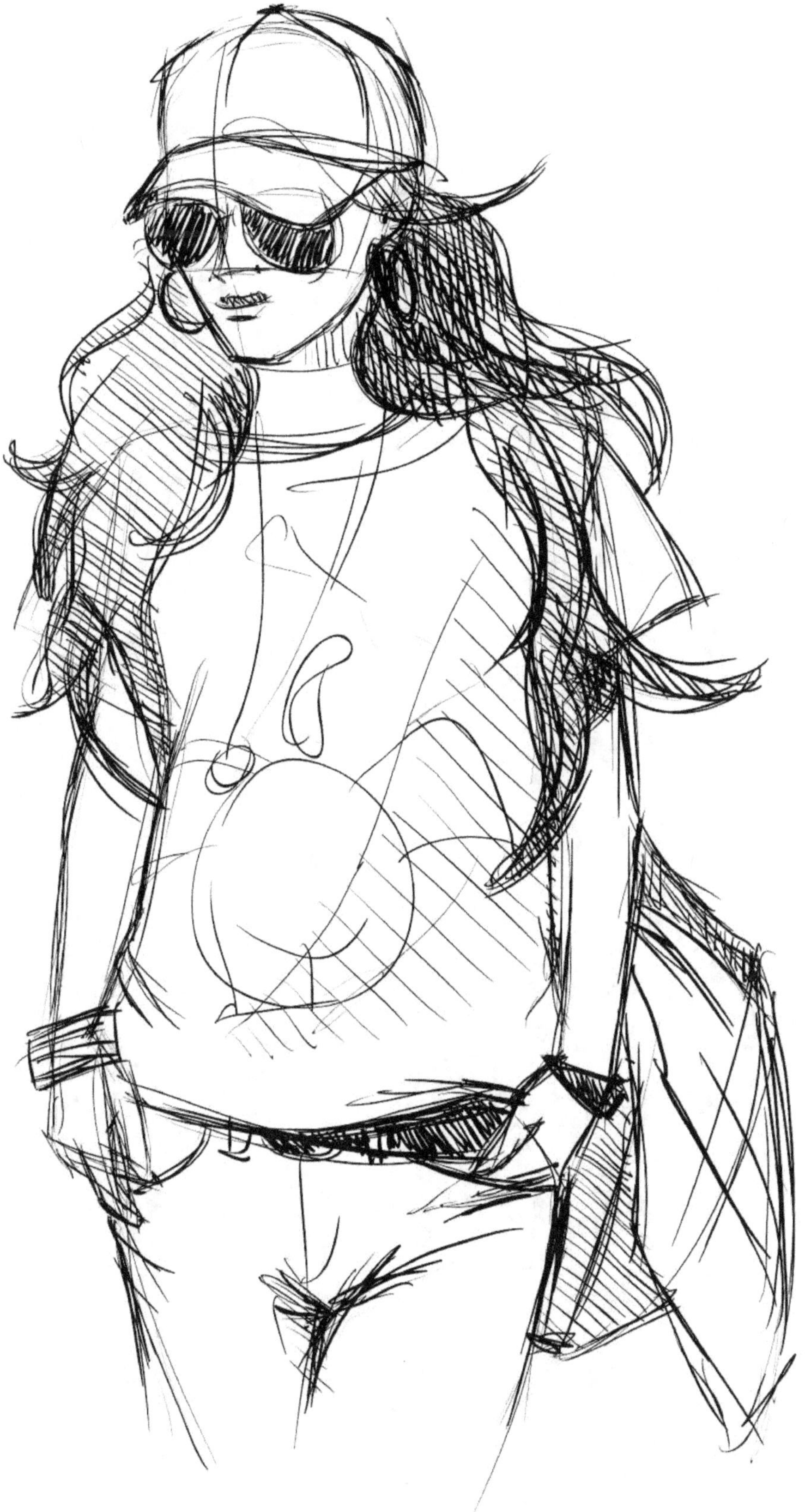

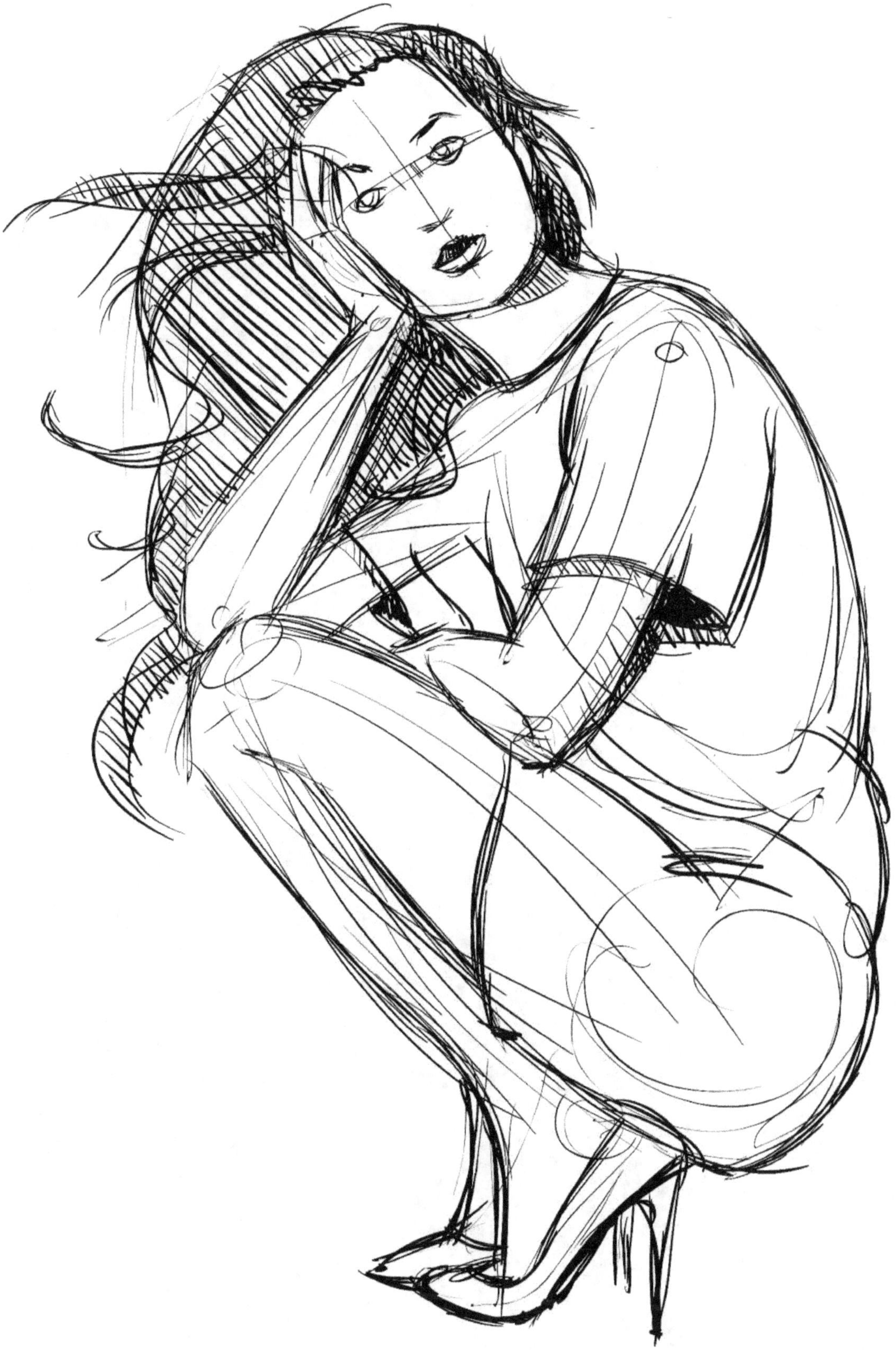

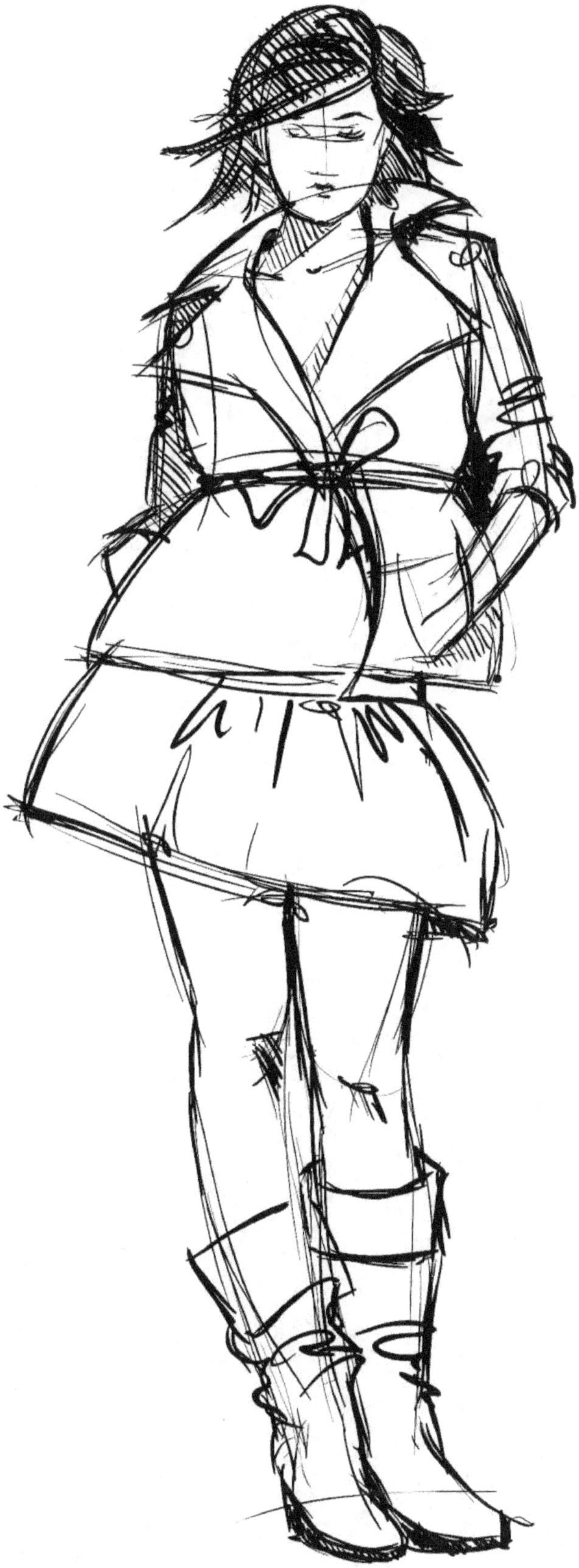

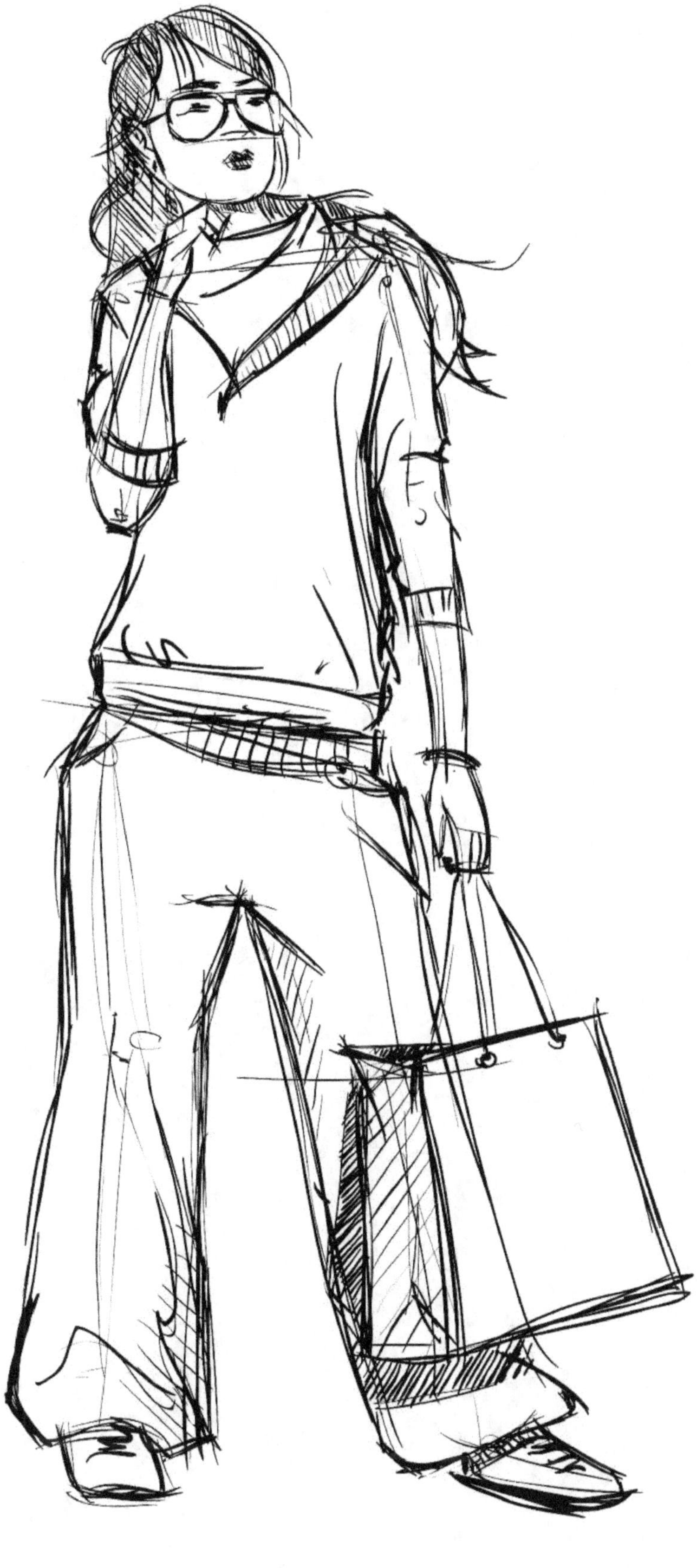

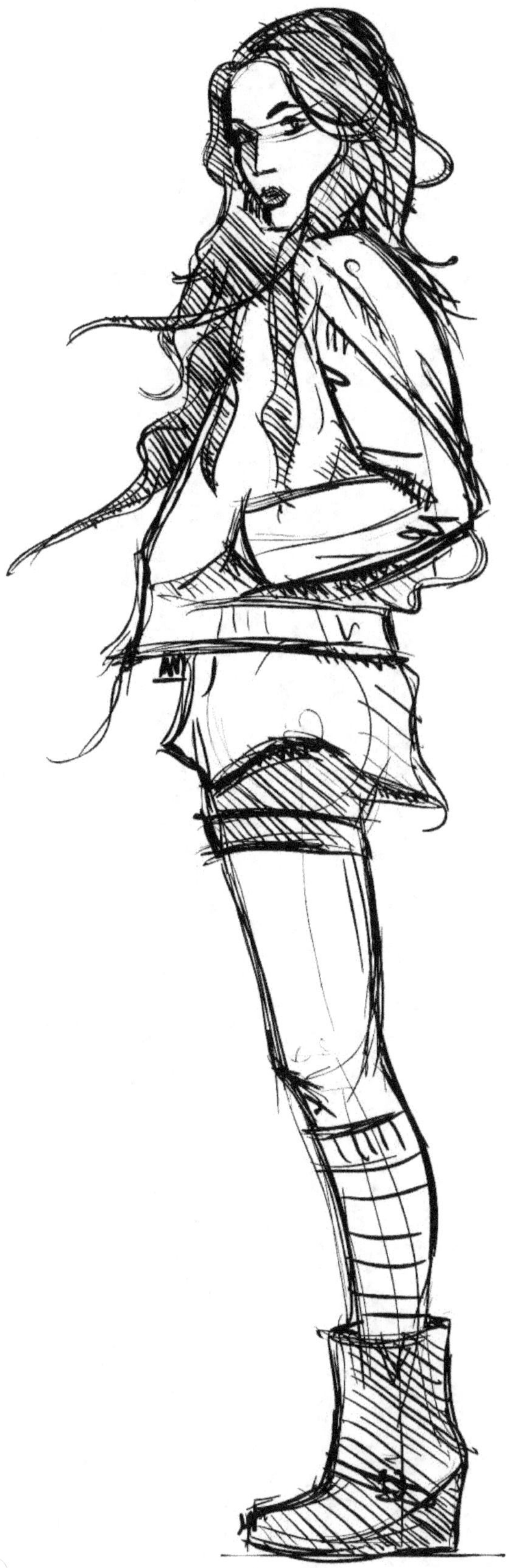

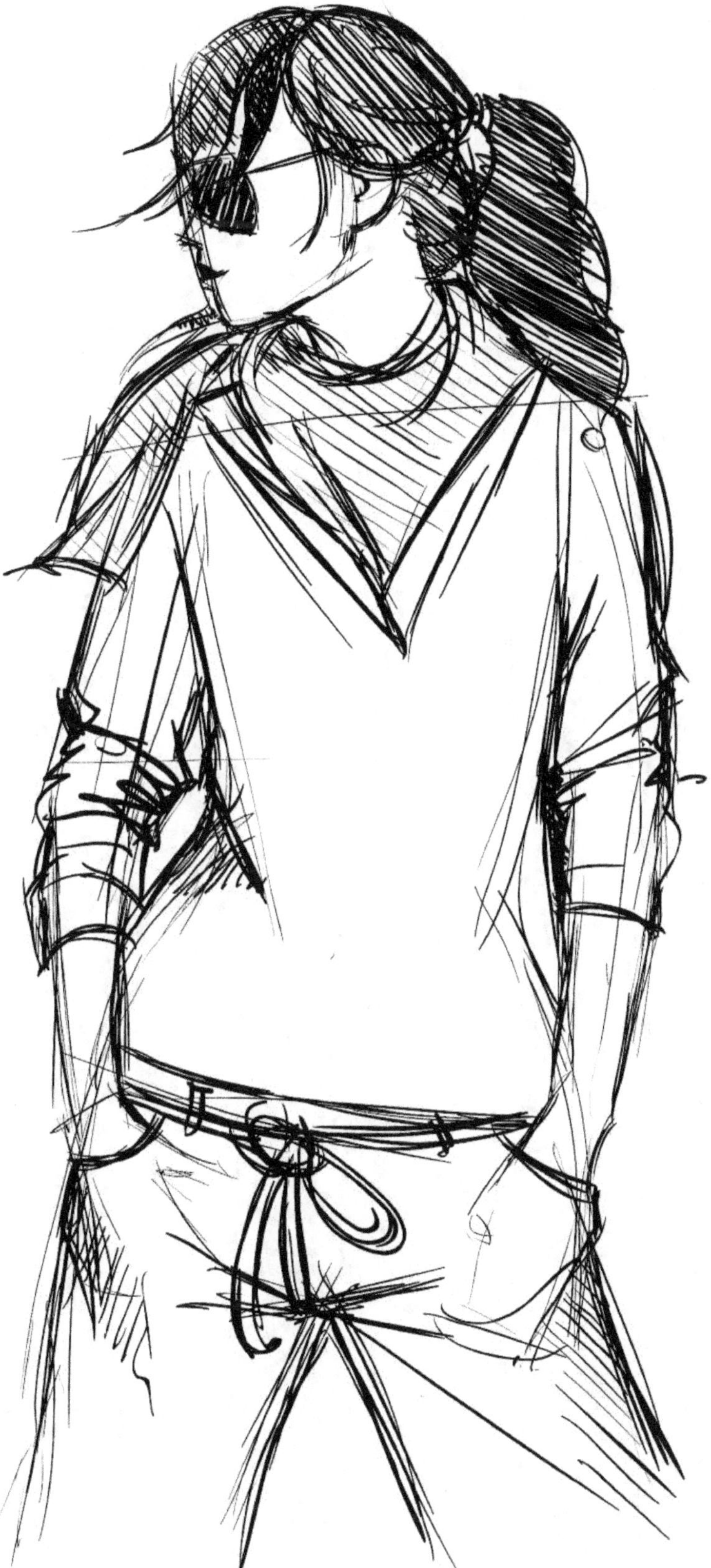

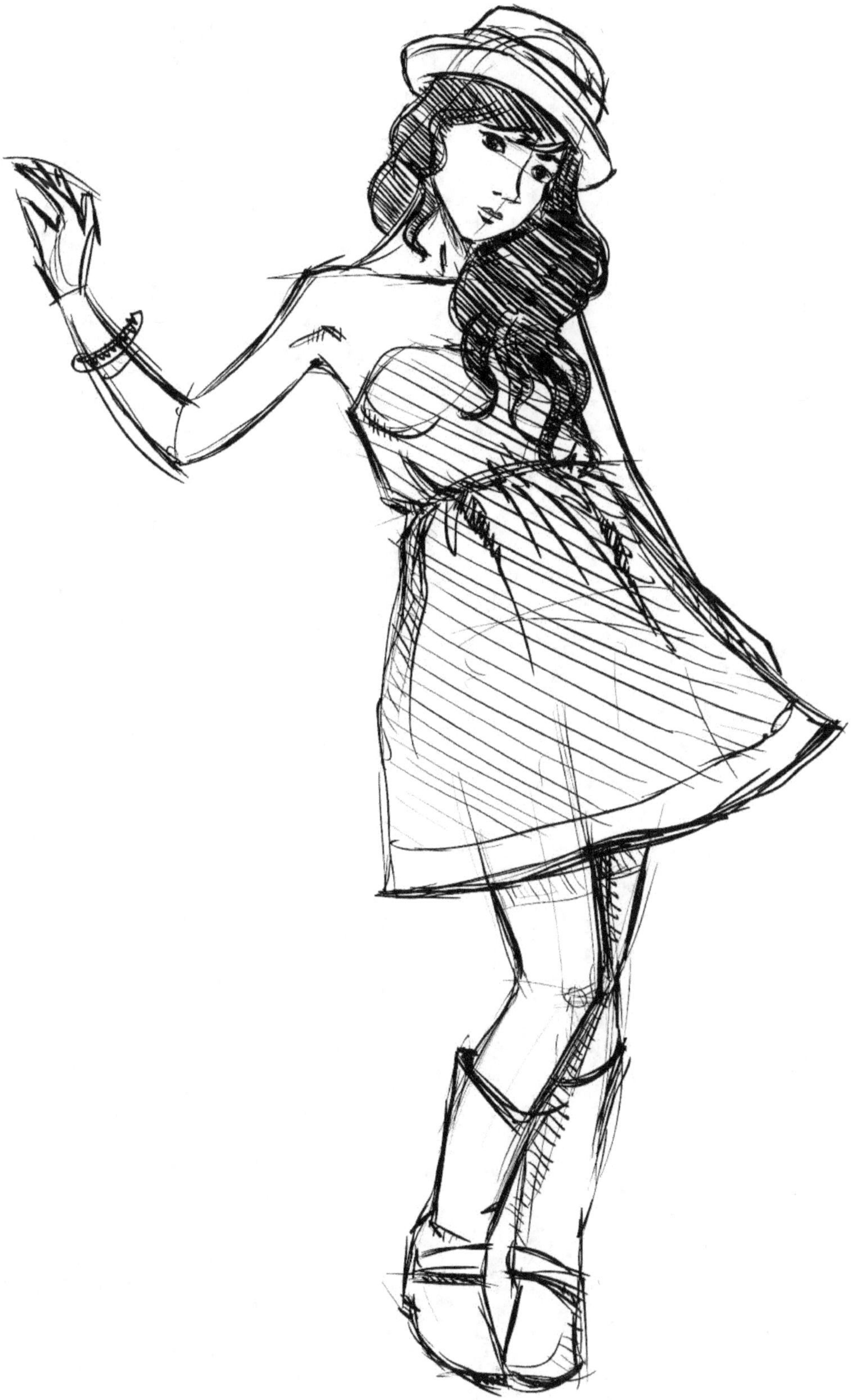

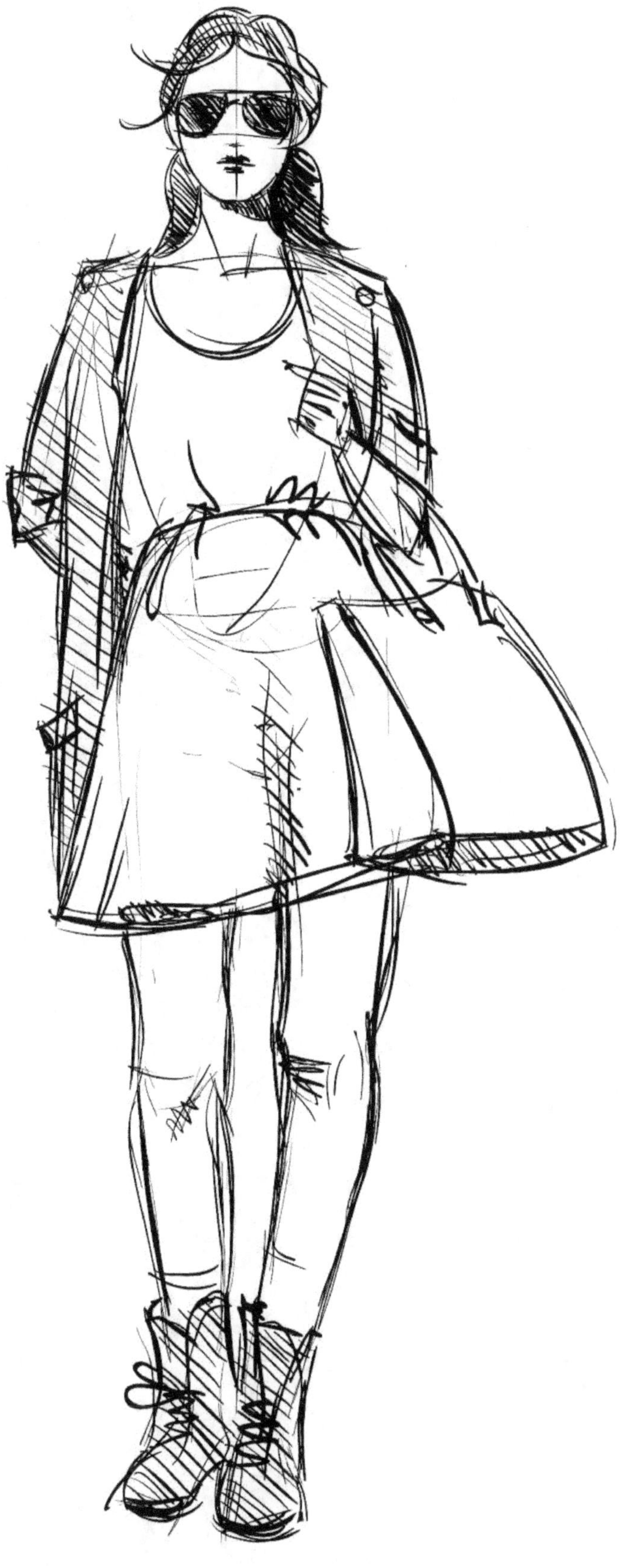

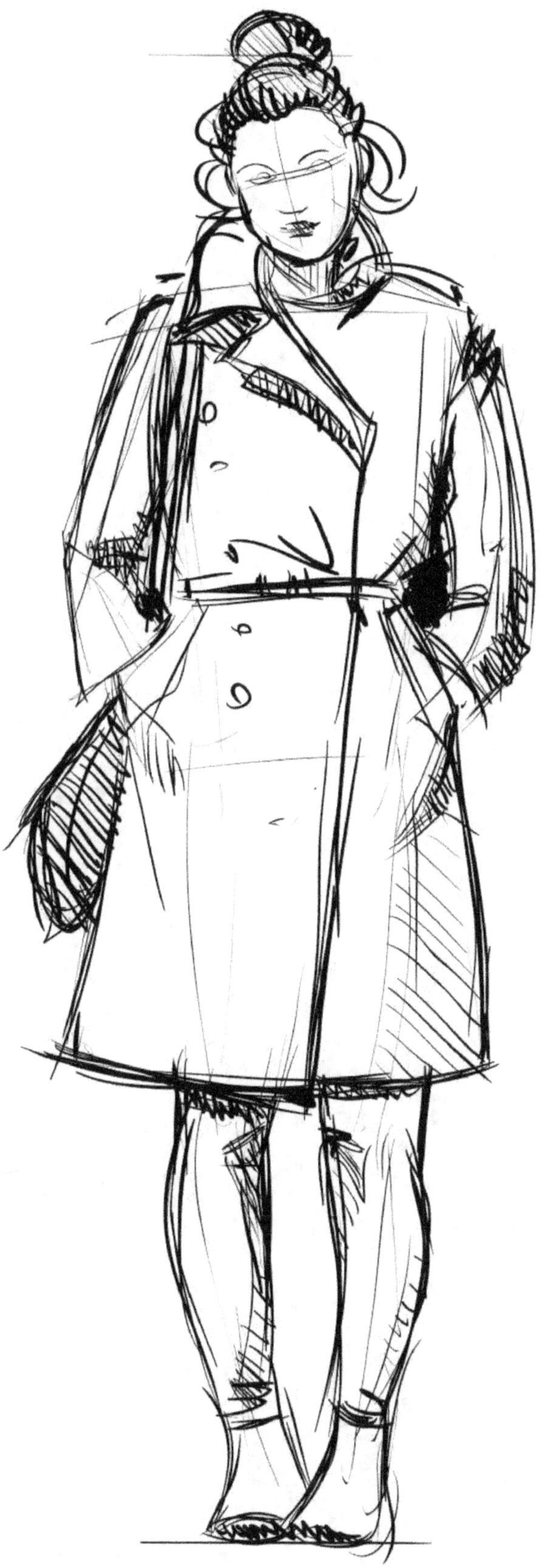

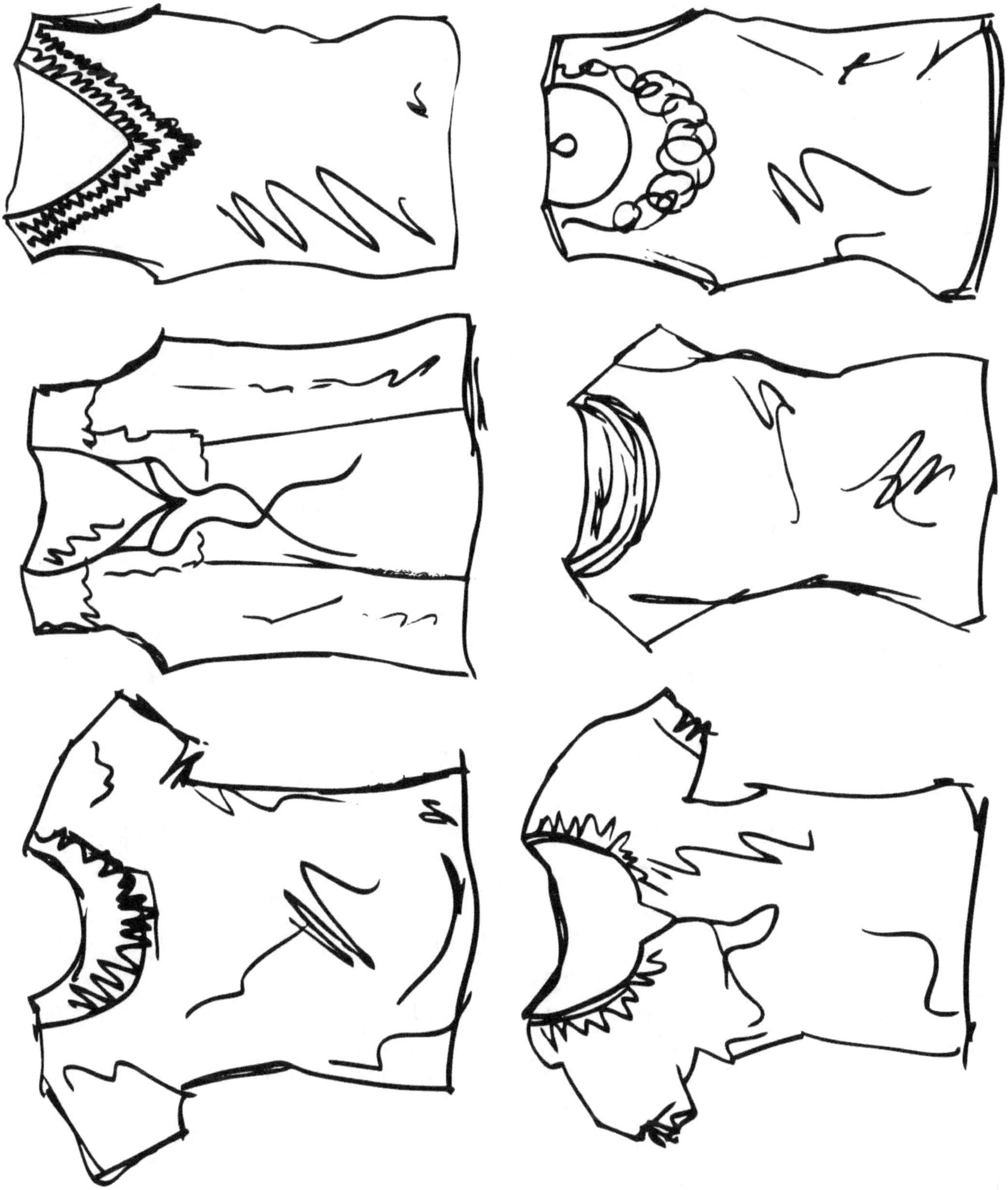

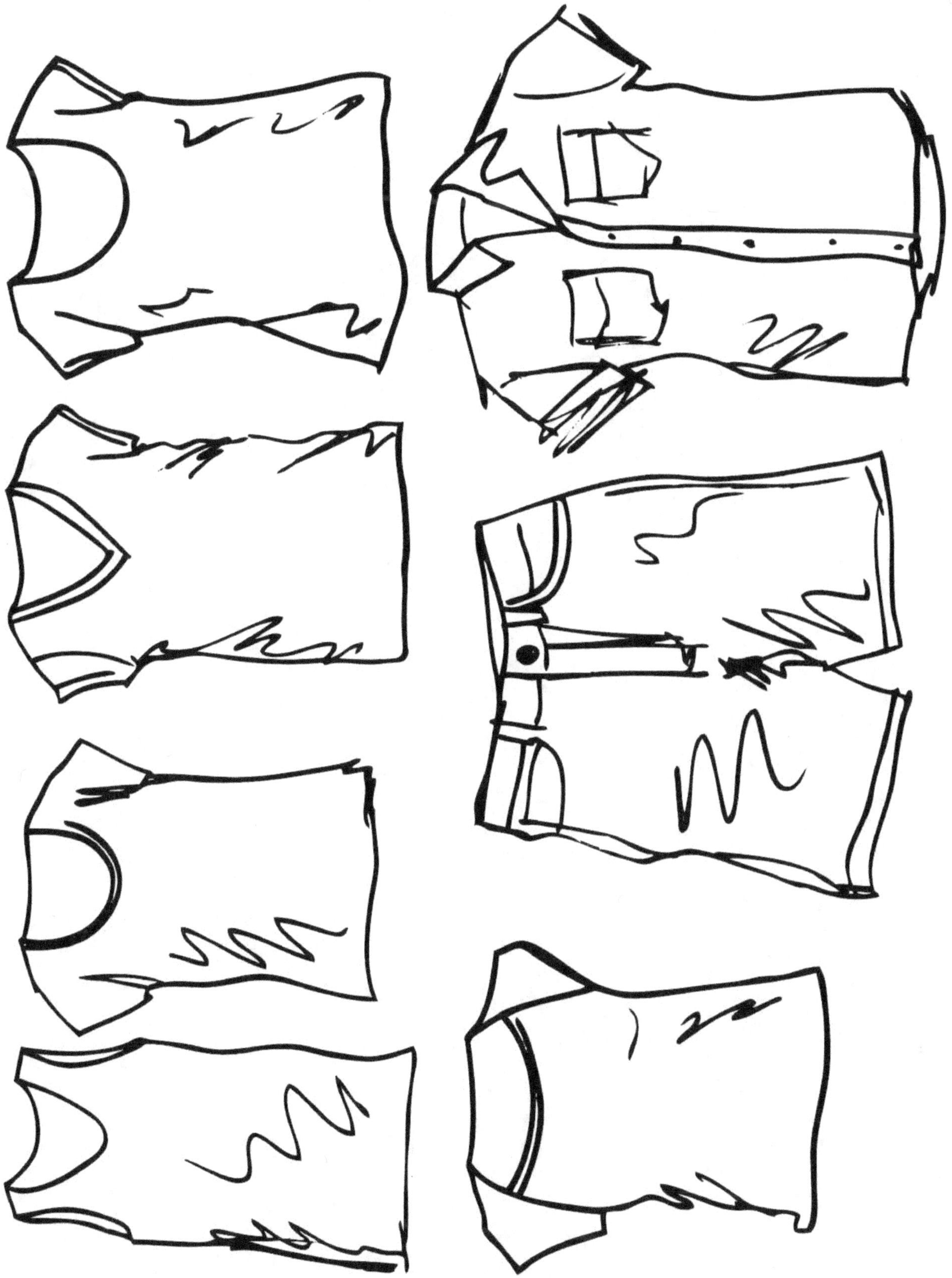

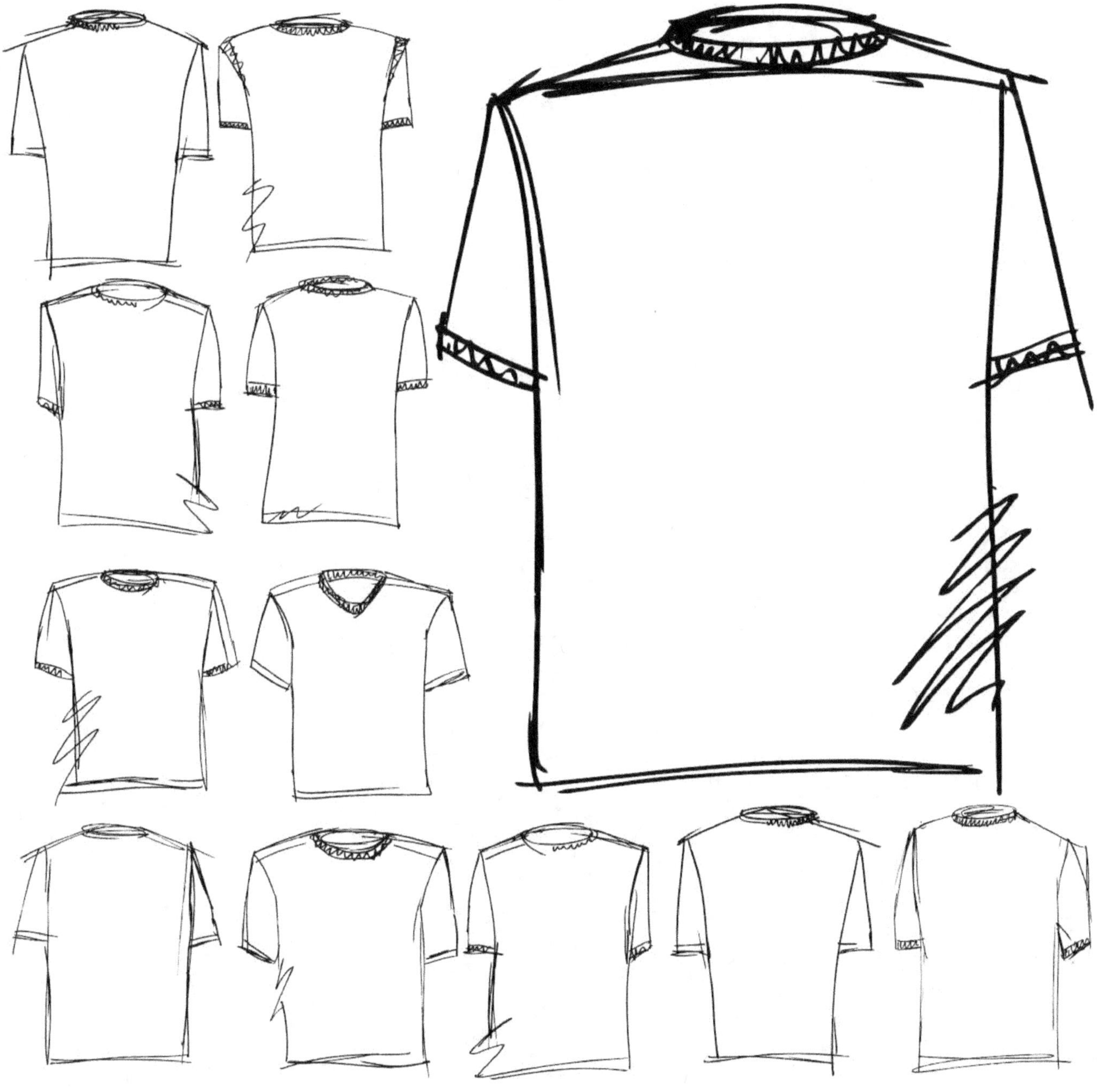

www.ingramcontent.com/pod-product-compliance
Lightning Source LLC
Chambersburg PA
CBHW081245280526
45787CB00006B/2803
* 9 7 8 1 5 3 5 1 6 4 9 5 5 *